Anna Madgigine
Jai Kingsley

Florida A&M University, Tallahassee
Florida Atlantic University, Boca Raton
Florida Gulf Coast University, Ft. Myers
Florida International University, Miami
Florida State University, Tallahassee
New College of Florida, Sarasota
University of Central Florida, Orlando
University of Florida, Gainesville
University of North Florida, Jacksonville
University of South Florida, Tampa
University of West Florida, Pensacola

Anna Madgigine Jai Kingsley

African Princess, Florida Slave, Plantation Slaveowner

Daniel L. Schafer

University Press of Florida

Gainesville · Tallahassee · Tampa · Boca Raton
Pensacola · Orlando · Miami · Jacksonville · Ft. Myers · Sarasota

Copyright 2003 by Daniel L. Schafer
Printed in the United States of America on acid-free paper
All rights reserved
First cloth printing, 2003
First paperback printing, 2010

18   17   16   15   14   13   6   5   4   3   2

Library of Congress Cataloging-in-Publication Data
Schafer, Daniel L.
Anna Madgigine Jai Kingsley: African princess, Florida slave,
plantation slaveowner / Daniel L. Schafer
p. cm.
Includes bibliographical references and index.
ISBN 9780-8130-2616-9 (cloth)
ISBN 978-0-8130-3554-3 (paper)
1. Kingsley, Anna, 1793–1870. 2. Women slaves—Florida—Fort George
Island—Biography. 3. Slaves—Florida—Fort George Island—Biography.
4. Princesses—Senegal—Biography. 5. Women plantation owners—
Florida—Fort George Island—Biography. 6. African American
women—Florida—Fort George Island—Biography. 7. Kingsley family.
8. Plantation life—Florida—Fort George Island. 9. Fort George Island
(Fla.)—Biography. 10. Senegal—Biography. I. Title.
E444.K56 S33 2003
975.9'12—dc21   2002033372

The University Press of Florida is the scholarly publishing agency
for the State University System of Florida, comprising Florida A&M
University, Florida Atlantic University, Florida Gulf Coast Univer-
sity, Florida International University, Florida State University, New
College of Florida, University of Central Florida, University of
Florida, University of North Florida, University of South Florida, and
University of West Florida.

University Press of Florida
15 Northwest 15th Street
Gainesville, FL 32611–2079
www.upf.com

Contents

Maps & Photographs

Maps

Photographs

Preface

The story of Anna Kingsley has long been the subject of speculation and rumor. In one legend Anna is described as a black woman from Madagascar; in another she is said to be of "Arabian" descent and mixed racial ancestry. One writer said Anna wore "a white turban" in Florida and described her as "tall, dignified, slender, with well formed features and a commanding presence."[1] After knowing her for nearly forty years, Zephaniah Kingsley, the ship captain and East Florida planter who purchased her as a slave in 1806 and later made her his wife, described her as "a fine, tall figure, black as jet, but very handsome."[2]

The most persistent legend identifies Anna Kingsley as the daughter of an African king who sold slaves to Kingsley and arranged to have a ship captain marry his daughter by providing a dowry consisting of numerous slaves. A journalist who visited Florida in 1878, nearly a decade after Anna Kingsley's death, heard from local residents that she was "an African princess twelve years of age [who] was presented to [Captain Kingsley] by her father. He brought her to America, gave her some little education, and took her to his bed and board without publication of the banns. At a later period, however, he carried her to Hayti and made her his legal wife. Ma'am Hannah, as she was called, bore him several children."[3]

Susan Philippa Fatio L'Engle, an educated white woman from one of the area's elite families, became Anna's friend and a frequent visitor to Fort George Island. Susan L'Engle's description of Anna as a lonely "African princess" prompted a family legend that has survived to the present.[4] Gertrude Rollins Wilson, whose father purchased Fort George Island after the Civil War, claimed that servants told her mother tales of an imperious Anna Madgigine Jai holding a mass meeting "every evening" when the laborers returned from the fields, at which time she would "read the penalties for the day, standing on the side porch while the crowd of slaves listened submissively."[5]

I once stood outside that house and heard a tour guide say that Anna Kingsley punished reluctant laborers by nailing their ears to a whipping post. A clergyman in the audience responded by citing Old Testament precedents for such cruel treatment. The memories are not always flattering or accurate, but long after Anna Kingsley moved away from the house she occupied at Fort George Island, it continued to be known as the "Princess House" and the "Ma'am Anna House."

Curiously, the "African princess" references may be the most credible of the Anna Kingsley stories, even though they cannot be conclusively proven. Most of the legends were rumors passed down through the decades by uncritical journalists and local historians who seldom checked for accuracy. Carita Doggett Corse, a local historian and the director of the Florida Writers' Program under the Works Progress Administration in the 1930s, wrote that Anna "insisted upon the oriental custom of waiting upon her husband's guests, because among Eastern women this has always been considered the privilege of a wife."[6] This characterization contradicts Corse's other comments depicting Anna as a regal and "dignified" woman with a "commanding presence," in unquestioned control of a slave plantation.

The image of a subservient Anna waiting on her husband and his guests was embraced by tour guides at Kingsley Plantation after it became a Florida Park Service site in 1955. Guides would gather visitors around a dining table in the owner's dwelling and dramatize an imaginary scene in which Anna stood behind her husband at mealtime fanning guests at the table while they dined. As they told this story, guides would pull a cord attached to a large fan of peacock feathers mounted on the ceiling above the table, much to the pleasure of perspiring visitors.

The National Park Service acquired Kingsley Plantation in 1991 and instituted research-based tour scripts. The peacock fan was removed and the "oriental custom" story was discontinued. To their dismay, park rangers continue to encounter repeat visitors who are disappointed to discover the fan missing and the "oriental custom" story in disrepute.

I first heard the legends in 1975. A tour guide talked excitedly about a controversial planter and ship captain who purchased enslaved laborers in Africa for his Florida estates. Several enslaved women became his conjugal partners and the mothers of his children. One of the women, the tour guide said, had special status as Kingsley's acknowledged wife because she was the daughter of an African king.

For days afterward I was haunted by this account. First, nothing was said about the African men and women who had occupied the tabby cabins we viewed. Further, the image of the daughter of an African king fanning her master and his guests at dinner, humbling herself in such a public way, failed to match a document the guide talked about that described her as a person of intelligence and dignity. It became clear that a serious investigation was needed and that the persons who once occupied Kingsley Plantation were linked to issues of surpassing importance in the history of the Atlantic world.

During the next several months I repeatedly visited Kingsley Plantation in order to become thoroughly familiar with the setting; then I talked to local nonvocational historians who were well versed in the story. After that I frequented local and regional libraries, archives, and courthouses, and then traveled along the Atlantic Coast as far as Nova Scotia searching for evidence concerning the Kingsley legends. Over the years I have continued the search in Great Britain, Denmark, the Dominican Republic, and St. Thomas, as well as the West African nations of Guinea and Senegal. It has taken nearly thirty years, but I have come to know the Kingsley family well enough to separate legend from fact and to fit their story into the broader histories of the African diaspora, Florida, and the United States.

My first effort to tell the story of Anna Kingsley was carried out in partnership with a newspaper reporter, Michael Nyenhuis, in a December 1993 series in the *Florida Times-Union*. That series, titled "Anna Jai," prompted the St. Augustine Historical Society to publish a brief monograph titled *Anna Kingsley* in July 1994. An expanded version appeared in 1997.[7]

This volume represents a significant departure from that earlier work. Less is said here about Zephaniah Kingsley. Anna's life story deserves to stand alone, without Zephaniah's larger-than-life shadow detracting from her importance. Examined for the first time are the legends depicting Anna Kingsley as an "African princess" and the fate of the Kingsley clan in Florida following Zephaniah's death in 1843. Also new is discussion of the Kingsley family's role in a rural community of whites, free blacks, and persons of mixed race that flourished in the 1840s and 1850s, despite the racist hysteria that accompanied the drive for secession from the Union.

My goal has been to write a lively and imaginative yet scholarly account that would appeal to general readers and professional historians alike. I want readers to become acquainted with the entire life of Anna Kingsley, including her childhood years in Africa and the events that led to her captivity and enslavement. It has been difficult to find hard evidence for Anna's early years in Senegal, where history was preserved in the memories of the trained oral historians known as griots, who were attached to the royal families. The body of information that remains is sometimes contradictory and incomplete.

This relates to a larger problem for historians studying African diaspora topics: It is seldom possible to find complete documentation for the lives of humans who were enslaved, transported across oceans and between nations, and who survived fires, wars, and the ravages of slavery. Recreating a life story as complicated as the one lived by Anna Kingsley without benefit of extensive documentation is methodologically challenging. Very few written observations by relatives or close personal friends have been found. If she kept a diary or wrote personal letters, they were apparently lost or destroyed. It became necessary, therefore, to borrow from accounts of documented parallel lives and from the extensive secondary literature concerning the Atlantic slave trade and slavery, while drawing informed inferences from a limited body of specific factual evidence. Historians must on occasion depend on reasonable and informed conjecture and be willing to tolerate a degree of uncertainty. Fortunately, there is a small but significant collection of secondary literature that interprets the history of free persons of color in the antebellum South. I have drawn on this literature repeatedly, especially the work of Ira Berlin, while trying to understand the actions and motivations of Anna Kingsley.[8]

Acknowledgments

This book would not have been possible without the assistance of kind friends and interested scholars and archivists. I have tried to remember all who helped by expressing my gratitude in endnotes.

Page L. Edwards, deceased now but for many years the executive director of the St. Augustine Historical Society, commissioned the 1994 monograph *Anna Kingsley* after reading the week-long "Anna Jai" series in the *Florida Times-Union*. Without that invitation and Page's continuing support, the story of Anna Kingsley would have languished in the obscurity of a forgotten newspaper series.

Svend E. Holsoe gave generous help in Copenhagen in November 1994, including helpful translations of Danish records and careful critical readings of drafts. Peter Sørensen, Per Nielsen, and Poul Olsen provided special assistance at the Danish National Archives. Bruce Chappell led me through the intricacies of the Spanish records at the P. K. Yonge Library of Florida History, while James Donlan helped with translations. Jane L. Landers sent relevant copies of Cathedral Parish Records, samples of her own scholarship, advice, and friendship. Jean Parker Waterbury and Kathy Tilford carefully read the manuscript at its various stages. Victoria Bomba Coifman, who trained me in African history, contributed information on Wolof names as well as ongoing help and encouragement.

A sabbatical leave from duties at the University of North Florida, along with professional development funds, made possible my 1994 research trip to West Africa. Brian Peters, then the Site Supervisor at Kingsley Plantation of the Timucuan Ecological and Historic Preserve (a National Park Service site), arranged grants from the Eastern National Parks and Monuments Association for research in Africa, Denmark, England, and the Dominican Republic. In Senegal essential advice was provided by Professors Mbaye Guèye, Mamadou Diouf, Penda Mbow, and Boubacar Barry of Cheikh Anta Diop University. Andre Zaiman and Katy Diop of the Gorée Institute arranged housing, meetings, and transportation.

At Puerto Plata, Dominican Republic, attorneys Neit Finke and Pablo Juan Brugal shared their knowledge of Dominican law and history and copies of rare documents. Tony and Sandra Lebrón treated me like family and arranged transportation and interviews with Kingsley descendants, while their son Manuel, like his mother a descendant of Anna Kingsley, translated. Peggy Fried later provided important documents from Dominican Republic archives.

The March 2000 Anna Kingsley in Senegal Historical Conference at Gorée Island produced several insights that have been incorporated into this volume. The conference was made possible by grants from the Division of Cultural Affairs, State of Florida, the Florida Humanities Council, and the University of North Florida. Professor Mbaye Guèye of Cheikh Anta Diop University was responsible for the planning and arrangements in Dakar. The Honorable Abdou Diouf, then President of Senegal, along with his Minister of Education, Andre Sanko, and Associate Minister, Dr. Sidi Camara, arranged for government permits and other support.

Finally, and above all, I thank Joan E. Moore, my wife, for working with me in the archives and helping edit the numerous drafts. For more than twenty years she has been my essential source of inspiration. Her love and support make most things possible for me.

Introduction

ON MARCH 4, 1811, an East Florida planter named
Zephaniah Kingsley, Jr., asked Spanish authorities to
issue emancipation papers for an enslaved "black
woman called Anna, around eighteen years of age,
bought as a bozal [newly arrived from Africa] in the
port of Havana from a slave cargo."[1] Kingsley praised
the "nicety and fidelity" and "good qualities" of the
young woman, and also freed her "three mulatto children: George, about 3 years 9 months, Martha, 20
months old, and Mary, one month old." Thirty years
later, Kingsley again praised Anna for her "truth,
honor, integrity, moral conduct [and] good sense" and
said "she has always been respected as my wife."[2]

Within a year of achieving freedom, Anna Madgigine Jai Kingsley (she used the names Madgigine and
Jai to perpetuate the memory of her mother and father) established a homestead of her own. After surviving captivity and enslavement in Africa, a harrow-
ing trip across the Atlantic Ocean in the hold of a slave
ship, and a brief period of enslavement in Florida, she
was once again free and securely situated on a five-acre
tract with a new dwelling and several outbuildings.
Ironically, this newly freed black woman had also become the owner of twelve slaves.

Soon after the homestead was established, however,
East Florida was endangered by the Patriot War of
1812–15, a series of destructive raids by insurgents and

bandits intent on overthrowing the Spanish colonial regime and abducting black persons to sell as slaves in Georgia. Anna protected herself and her children heroically by torching all the buildings on the property, thereby denying shelter to her enemies, and then seeking safety on a Spanish gunboat.

In 1814 Anna and Zephaniah Kingsley began a twenty-five-year residency on Fort George Island, an Atlantic barrier island located near the mouth of the St. Johns River. Anna and Zephaniah's three children grew to maturity and married during these years, and a fourth child, John Maxwell Kingsley, was born. Fort George Island would be the setting for the only prolonged period of tranquility that Anna Kingsley would know in her life.

But that place of refuge was endangered when another threat to her freedom developed. In 1838 Kingsley transported Anna and her son John Maxwell to Haiti to escape the discriminatory racial practices instituted by the Americans after they gained control of Florida in 1821. In Haiti, a black republic formed in 1804 when enslaved Africans overthrew their French rulers, Zephaniah purchased a huge rural tract and established an agricultural colony in partnership with his and Anna's eldest son, George.

Eight years later Anna was back in Florida. Following Zephaniah's death in 1843, one of his sisters had sued to disinherit all Kingsley heirs of African ancestry. Anna returned to lead the family's fight to retain control of Zephaniah's extensive Florida properties. The racial odds were stacked against her, but the Florida courts decided in her favor.

After the trial concluded, Anna Kingsley remained in the United States and became the matriarch of the Kingsley clan in Florida. She purchased a small farm located between the plantation residences of her two daughters and helped found a unique free black community on the eastern shore of the St. Johns River, across from Jacksonville. In 1860 seventy free persons of color lived there, most of them Kingsley kinfolk or their former slaves. The community flourished for a time, withstanding the racist climate that accompanied the states' rights and secessionist fever dominating southern politics during the 1850s.

The inevitable outcome of all that turmoil—secession and war—

occurred in 1861. Finding no safety in the pro-slavery Confederate States of America, Anna Kingsley and her family fled to the Union states in April 1862.

After peace returned to northeast Florida in 1865, Anna returned with her daughters to what remained of their estates. Her wealth, like the fortunes of the entire Kingsley clan in Florida, had vanished. She resided with one of her daughters, holding on to life during a half-decade of declining fortunes and the deaths of several of those close to her. Finally came her own death.

In May or June 1870, Anna Madgigine Jai Kingsley died. She was buried in a family cemetery behind the dwelling of her daughter, Mary Kingsley Sammis. Anna Kingsley's final place of refuge is an unmarked grave in a peaceful grove in the Arlington area of Jacksonville, Florida. Nearby are the burial places of her daughters and grandchildren.

1 · Senegal

Anta Majigeen Ndiaye

THE EARLY YEARS of Anna Kingsley were tragically linked to the wars and slave raids that ravaged the Senegambia region of West Africa for centuries. This was especially true in the eighteenth and early nineteenth centuries for the Wolof states of Senegal, where Anna Kingsley, known then as Anta Majigeen Ndiaye, lived until she was captured and enslaved in 1806. Wars and slaving raids were so frequent that one of Senegal's most respected historians, Professor Mbaye Guèye, has called these years a period of great crisis for all of Senegambia.[1]

External wars between the Wolof states, the dominant ethnic group in Senegal, and the Fula people of Fuuta Tooro, or the Trarza emirates to the north, had been fought for most of the eighteenth century. Wars between the Wolof states were also frequent, with Kajoor alternately attacking Waalo, Jolof, and Bawol, or fending off their attacks. Rural villages were destroyed, and their residents dispersed or enslaved, with sufficient frequency that housing styles and village designs were transformed for protection against the recurring violence. Internal civil wars and dynastic disputes further disrupted normal social and political life in the region.[2]

Raids to capture slaves were endemic prior to the

arrival of Europeans at West African coastal ports in the fifteenth century. Captives of war were incorporated into villages as laborers or sent north to Arab and Berber outposts to exchange for trade goods. The most prized trade items were the swift and superior Arabian and Barbary horses of North Africa, which permitted the cavalry of powerful nations to terrorize and plunder their rivals. But the arrival of Portuguese traders at the coast and at the Cape Verde Islands brought unceasing demands for enslaved Africans that greatly increased the level of violence and ultimately destroyed the political stability of the region.[3]

When the Portuguese arrived at Senegambia in the fifteenth century, the Empire of Jolof (1200–1550) controlled the lands between the Senegal and Gambia Rivers. In the mythic traditions of Jolof, the empire was founded by Njaajaan Ndiaye, a Pulaar-speaking migrant from an Islamic state to the north who settled in the lower Senegal Valley among fractious Wolof speakers in control of local lands. Through wise leadership, this mythological outsider brought peace and the Islamic religion to the region and unified the local people. As Buurba Jolof (king of Jolof), Njaajaan Ndiaye established a capital near the Ferlo River in the interior of the region amid important trade routes, laying the foundation for a state that became the empire of Jolof.[4]

Four Wolof states emerged under the empire: Jolof, Kajoor, Bawol, and Waalo, with only Jolof located in the interior. As European coastal trade increased, the Wolof states with direct access to the Atlantic ports gained power from their ability to exchange grain and human captives for firearms, gunpowder, and other trade goods. The coastal states tired of paying tribute to Jolof and rebelled. By the eighteenth century, Jolof was the weaker of the four Wolof states.[5]

Successive rulers of Kajoor profited further from the coastal trade by expanding production of grain and other foodstuffs to sell to ship captains whose profits depended on keeping their human cargoes alive during the passage to the Americas. Other Wolof states also increased grain production and raided Bambara, Sereer, and other African nations located to the east and south to acquire laborers. Rivalries increased, and wars between the Wolof states were intermittent throughout the eighteenth century. Kajoor emerged as the dominant

Map 1. Senegambia, the land between the Senegal and Gambia rivers, showing the Wolof states of the eighteenth and nineteenth centuries. Yang Yang, an ancient capital of kings of Jolof, is believed to have been Anna Kingsley's home prior to 1806.

Wolof state by 1790 under the leadership of the Damel (king) of Kajoor, Amari Ngoone Ndella.[6]

The Damel's power depended on the much-feared tyeddo warriors, a caste of royal slaves owing allegiance only to Ndella. The tyeddo were in reality a standing army of professional soldiers, fierce and skilled cavalrymen who rode superior Arabian horses purchased by exchanging slaves captured in raids throughout the region. With little regard for Wolof villagers, the tyeddo plundered at will and escalated the level of violence. Writing about the establishment of warrior states, Boubacar Barry observed: "*Ceddo* [tyeddo] monarchies established violence as the determinant value, not only in relations between Senegambia's states, but also in political and social relations within each state."[7]

The crisis of the Wolof states heightened between 1790 and 1809, when internal religious wars broke out in Kajoor. An Englishman who saw the effects of the violence during these years described the villages on the Senegal River as still abandoned in 1811, the residents having been "carried into captivity and those who remain are constantly subjected to the plunder."[8] Professor Brahim Diop and other historical geographers in Senegal have discovered the remains of dozens of rural villages that were deserted as a result of the incessant violence. Diop concludes that the countryside was ravaged and the residents either captured or forced to flee for protection.[9] Anta Majigeen Ndiaye's years in Senegal, from 1793 to 1806, coincided with an intensely violent period in a long series of wars and slave raids.

Most Wolof people had converted to Islam long before the violence intensified in 1790. The leaders of many rural villages were Muslim clerics whose followers were pious farmers, fond of quiet family life and agricultural labor. Forbidden by their Islamic faith to imbibe alcohol or engage in sinful acts, they had grown resentful of the immorality of the ruling families. The hard-drinking, flamboyant, and violent tyeddo warriors were especially troublesome for the Muslim Wolof. The tyeddo were expected to attack only non-Wolof people, but when supplies of luxury goods or weapons ran low, the Damel and his agents overlooked raids on distant and unsuspecting Wolof villages.[10]

As Ndella's repression worsened, thousands of Muslim Wolof fled south and west to form their own state at the Cape Verde peninsula, enclosing their families in walled villages for protection against the tyeddo cavalrymen. But Ndella's warriors pursued relentlessly, crushing the rebellion and selling thousands of prisoners as slaves. The victims were exchanged for cloth, liquor, and luxury goods, and, more importantly, the guns and gunpowder necessary to resupply the Kajoor war machine.

The violence spread beyond the borders of Kajoor to pit one Wolof state against another, and draw even the non-Wolof Fula of Fuuta Tooro into the fighting. Warfare was suspended in most of Senegal in 1806, but the tyeddo continued to raid into Jolof as punishment for that state's previous support of Fuuta Tooro. In 1806 Ndella's soldiers brought many Wolof captives from Jolof to the coastal slave markets.[11]

Slaving raids were generally mounted between October and April, after the annual June to September rainy season ended and the muddy roads leading to the interior had dried. For raids conducted in March, rain would not have fallen for five months, sometimes longer. At this time of year, the intense sunlight and hot northerly winds blowing in from the Sahara Desert force the Zebu humped cattle to seek whatever shade they can find in the arid afternoons. Beside the roads stubbled fields of millet with wilted stalks stand parched and scratchy in the searing sun after the harvest.[12]

The fierce-looking tyeddo warriors would travel in the cool of the night, spurring their horses north and east into the dry and barren landscape of Jolof, stirring clouds of dust that settled on the long braided hair and firearms of the riders and coated the leaves of the acacia trees beside the narrow roadway. Wearing cloths over their faces for protection from the choking dust, the warriors rode on toward the dark and leafless limbs of baobob trees stretching to the Ferlo River and beyond, toward the middle reaches of the Senegal River.[13]

In 1806 mounted warriors converged on dozens of villages in Jolof, using stealth and the cover of darkness to conceal their destructive intentions. In the pre-dawn hours, horses pawed restlessly in the sand and scrub beyond the millet fields surrounding the villages, their riders waiting for the signal to attack. If an alert was sounded, residents would flee into the countryside seeking shelter in whatever woodlands remained to protect them from cavalry. The heavily forested regions that European travelers observed in the 1750s were beginning to disappear from the region by the early nineteenth century.[14] Too often, however, villagers awoke to the terrifying sounds of charging horses and the shouts of warriors as they burst into the family compounds.

Men, women, and children were seized, and objects of value were pillaged from the dwellings. Several men were killed as a warning that further resistance would be futile. The captives were fastened into chains or wooden fetters, formed into columns, and prodded to begin the long march toward the coast. Behind them smoke rose from the fires set by the looters, and bodies lay in the dust. For most of the captives, this would be the last memory of their African homes.

With fetters and yokes chafing and cutting, the captives trudged for days along dusty roads until the column reached the coast. Gener-

1. A baobob tree grows with wilted grass along the road to Yang Yang, an ancient capital of the empire of Jolof. The photo was taken by Joan E. Moore in March 2000, the dry season in Senegal.

ally, slave coffles arrived at the coastal ports of Senegal with two or three male captives for every female in the ranks, reflecting the demand for strong, young male workers in the Americas as well as the general preference for female over male slaves at the internal markets throughout Africa. Only during major wars between nations or severe famines would the convoys reaching the coastal markets include high ratios of women.[15]

Most slaves exported from Senegal left from St. Louis, an island in the mouth of the Senegal River. In 1806, however, enslaved victims of the tyeddo raids were rerouted to Gorée Island, another important export center. Major Richard Lloyd, the British commandant at Gorée, reported in 1805 that the French garrison at St.-Louis had been depleted by warfare with "some of the Native Princes on the River, with whom there is no probability of being on peaceful terms."[16] French raids in 1804, which Lloyd characterized as "indiscriminate plunder" to obtain slaves without permitting friends and relatives to redeem them, were blamed for the violent African attacks.

2. Cattle seek shelter from the sun during the long dry season in Senegal.
Photo by Joan E. Moore in March 2000.

In 1806 Lloyd reported that a thousand Africans were available for purchase at Gorée every year.[17]

Slave coffles stopped at Rufisque, located on the mainland across from Gorée. Today Rufisque is an obscure suburb of Dakar, the capital of Senegal, but in the early nineteenth century it was an important market town. An agent representing the Damel of Kajoor was in control of all slave sales at the market, a commerce that generated considerable income for the ruling family.[18]

At the Rufisque market, buyers could walk among captives to judge their strength and health. Those purchased were placed in long, narrow canoes that were pushed into the water and paddled toward the tip of Cape Verde, the westernmost point on the African continent. The vessels skirted the coastline for a distance before turning south into the open waters of a huge bay off the Atlantic Ocean. Two miles offshore was the island of Gorée, a narrow upthrust of basaltic rock only a few hundred yards wide and less than a mile long, with steep cliffs facing the mainland.[19]

The remote and fortified stronghold known to European traders as Gorée (from the Dutch word for good harbor) had been home to slave merchants since the middle of the fifteenth century. Portuguese nationals controlled the island and its trade until 1627, when the

Dutch seized and settled it in order to facilitate a supply of slave labor for their American colonies. A French naval expedition drove the Dutch from Gorée in 1677, and control thereafter passed back and forth primarily between the French and English. Under French dominance, Gorée became a thriving trade post sought out by captains from all European nations in search of provisions, good water, and human cargo. Gorée Island was controlled by the British from 1800 until 1817.[20]

Canoes arriving at Gorée rounded an arm of land that sheltered a snug harbor. A shore party pulled the slender vessels onto the soft sand beach and led the captives up a slight incline and along narrow streets. Captives then entered padlocked courtyards enclosed by high stone walls, or were led into long, windowless rooms where chains and manacles lined the dank walls.[21]

For generations enslaved Africans passed through Gorée's holding pens. Men, women, and children, their total number lost through the centuries of the slave trade, were chained in basement dungeons beneath the spacious homes of the merchants who purchased and re-sold them to Europeans. As many as twelve hundred captives could be chained at a time in Gorée's dungeons and adjoining courtyard

3. Gorée Island, two miles from Dakar, Senegal, functioned for centuries as a slave depot and fortified stronghold for European colonial powers. Photo by the author, November 1994.

4. The protected harbor and sand beach on Gorée Island where canoes from the mainland arrived with enslaved men and women. Photo by Joan E. Moore, March 2000.

prisons. Destined for the holds of European ships and then for slavery in the Americas, African captives who reached Gorée remained only until the next European ships arrived.[22]

Many enslaved victims perished before the ships departed. The Chevalier de Boufflers, governor of Senegal in the 1780s, complained of one consequence of disposing of the bodies of these victims in the waters surrounding the island: "At the moment, the air of Senegal is at its worst. Imagine that we smell from our bedrooms, and especially from mine, the stench of the corpses of the captives who die in their dozens in the dungeons and which the traders, in order to economize, throw in the water with cannonballs attached to their feet. The cannonballs eventually falling off; the bodies float between the waves and end up on the shore in places that one can reach neither on foot nor by boat; they remain among the palm trees and gradually rot."[23]

Governor Boufflers married a famous *signare* of Gorée, Anne Pépin, the daughter of a French naval surgeon and a mixed-race African woman. The governor built two houses for Pépin and left her with wealth and influence when he returned to France in 1789. *Signares* (from the Portuguese word for lady, *senhora*) were important merchants at Gorée for several generations. European merchants and government officials who came to the island arrived without their wives and soon formed quasi-legal liaisons with African women that were sanctioned by a *marriage à la mode du pays* (traditional marriage ceremony of the country). Children born of the relationships were given the names of their fathers, who seldom stayed long at Gorée. Those who died or returned to their white wives in France often left businesses in the hands of their African mates, the *signares* of Gorée, who became the female heads of "canoe companies" that dominated coastal trade and island commerce with Europeans.[24]

James Searing characterizes the *signares* as pioneer business-women who provided European merchants with a wide range of goods and services, including slaves sold at mainland markets. The *signares* themselves owned large numbers of slaves, who filled labor needs on the island and operated the canoes needed for the coastal trade. The families of mulatto merchants who descended from the *signares* became the essential middle-level arbiters in the slave trade to Gorée and St.-Louis.[25]

Below the expansive residences of the *signares*, thousands of en-

5. Stone walls on Gorée Island enclose courtyards where slaves were imprisoned. The island's prison cells held up to 1,200 men and women destined for slavery in the Americas. Photo by the author, November 1994.

6. This home was built in 1771 for the *signare* Victoria Albis, a mixed-race woman who headed a canoe company that purchased slaves on the mainland. Photo by the author, November 1994.

slaved captives were locked in windowless dungeons. Light came into the prison rooms only when guards brought food and water. At some point in their confinement, the captives were brought out and paraded before European buyers. After prices were agreed upon, the captives were led back to the dark prison cells. Meanwhile, offshore ships rode at anchor as barrels of water, food, and other items were loaded into the crowded holds beneath the decks. Also aboard were huge iron cooking pots and assorted utensils necessary to prepare food during the dangerous ocean crossing that lay ahead. Once the ships were loaded and prepared, the captives were led to canoes in the harbor.

Waves rocked the canoes tumultuously as the human cargoes were loaded. Unfamiliar faces peered from the ships' decks, the faces of white men who shouted in a strange language and hurried the captives through an opening on the deck and down into noise, confusion, and darkness. The wooden half-bunks protruding from the sides of the ship three feet below the deck would be their beds during the ocean crossing. Many terror-filled days and weeks lay ahead.

It is believed that Anta Majigeen Ndiaye was captured during one of the tyeddo raids into Jolof in 1806. The evidence, it must be said, is circumstantial. It is based first on Anna Kingsley's statement in Florida that she was from Senegal, and also on her continuing use of the names Madgigine and Jai (Majigeen and Ndiaye in Wolof) throughout her life in the Americas. It is known that she arrived in Florida in November 1806, and that her age then was thirteen years. In Florida a legend persists that Anna Kingsley had been a "royal princess" in Africa prior to her enslavement. In addition, a legend persists among Wolof people at Yang Yang, an ancient capital of Jolof, that seems to link Anna Madgigine Jai Kingsley to a daughter of the ruling Ndiaye lineage who was an unsuccessful contender for the position of Buurba Jolof. The name of the daughter given in the Jolof legend is Anta Majigeen Ndiaye.[26]

Based on her age at the time she was emancipated in Florida, Anta Majigeen Ndiaye was born in 1793, during the reign of Mba Kompas Ndiaye, who was Buurba Jolof from 1762 to 1797. Vincent Monteil, the author of respected studies of lines of succession of Buurba Jolofs, lists Mba Kompas as the thirteenth ruler, although it should be said that compilers often disagree on positions in the line of succession and on dates of rule. Mba Kompas's successor, Mba Buri-Nyabu, is believed to have held power for approximately thirty-five years,

7. The dungeons at "La Maison des Esclaves" (the slaves' house) on Gorée once held enslaved captives of war. Built ca. 1786 by the African descendants of a French naval surgeon. Photo by the author, November 1994.

circa 1798–1833. During his tenure, incessant and violent dynastic disputes as well as wars between the Wolof states devastated the towns in Jolof.[27]

Abdou Cissé, a griot (local historian) who still commands respect in the vicinity of Yang Yang, an ancient capital of Jolof, for his knowledge of the former rulers of the kingdom, believes that Anta Majigeen Ndiaye's father was a member of the royal lineage. Abdou is the son of Saliou Cissé, the official griot for Buurba Bouna Albouri Ndiaye, the last ruler of Jolof. Abdou Cissé maintains that at some time between 1797 and 1806, Anta's father contended for power in a bitter dynastic dispute within the Ndiaye patrilineage, a common occurrence during those years of crisis. Anta's father was the loser. His life was spared, but he was sent into exile, banished from home and family carrying only a gun and a sack of possessions on his back. His wives, children, slaves, and other properties were confiscated.[28]

Further elaboration was given in a May 2000 interview with Abdou Cissé conducted at Dahra, Senegal, by Ababacar Sy, professor of English at the regional school. The griot identified Anta Majigeen Ndiaye as a daughter of a contender for the throne, and then said, "The family of Anta Madgiguéne doesn't want to say that Anta

8. This Wolof family compound is located in contemporary Dahra, Senegal, a regional trade center in the heart of the old state of Jolof. The husband lives in the dwelling on the right; the other structures are for his wives and children. Photo by Joan E. Moore, March 2000.

9. A village elder at Yang Yang, an ancient capital of kings of Jolof. Photo by Joan E. Moore, March 2000.

Madjiguéne was a slave. This seems to be a dishonour in the family. For the family, Anta Madjiguéne had traveled in 1807 and hadn't come back. They didn't know more about her."[29] The griot, as a representative of the former ruling family, chose a discreet way to say that Anta was either captured and enslaved or sold into slavery by the family. Mr. Sy's own judgment is that "the real truth is" that Anta, "like many Senegalese or African people," was enslaved and "deported to abroad."[30]

In March 2000 I heard a similar account from elders of the village of Yang Yang. Anta, the elders said, was born in their village, and her father was a direct descendant of Njaajaan Ndiaye. A privileged daughter of a man of noble lineage, Anta was reared in a stratified society of nobles, free farmers, and slaves. That changed, however, when her father led an unsuccessful contest for the kingship.[31]

It is not possible to date that challenge precisely. It may have happened following the death of Mba Kompas in 1797, or it may have been one of many unsuccessful challenges to the rule of Mba Buri-

Nyabu after 1798. The griot stated that two of Anta's brothers survived the violence of the dynastic dispute that drove their father into exile, and later came back to Yang Yang to lead successful military challenges that brought their branch of the family into power. Judging from the lines of succession traced by Oumar Ndiaye Leyti and Vincent Monteil, which are based on a number of griot accounts collected in the first half of the twentieth century, the brothers may have been the eighteenth and twenty-second Buurba Jolofs, Lat-Kodu Majigeen Ndiaye and Birayamb Majigeen Ndiaye, rulers in the mid-nineteenth century. Anta would have been in her fifties by then, a widow living in Florida and unaware that two of her brothers were the current rulers of the strife-ridden homeland from which she had been forcefully separated more than four decades before.[32]

Mamadou Diouf, a historian from Senegal, has speculated that at some point during Anta Majigeen Ndiaye's enslavement in Senegal, she may have been recognized as the child of a noble family and brought into the household of one of the *signares* of Gorée. If that is

10. Abdou Cissé, a griot (oral historian) whose ancestors memorized the history of the rulers of the empire of Jolof. The drum was made by his great-grandfather, Saliou Cissé, a griot at Yang Yang. Photo by Joan E. Moore, March 2000.

11. Wolof girls at Yang Yang. Anta Majigeen Ndiaye (later Anna Madgigine Jai Kingsley) was nearly the age of the girl on the right when she was captured during a slave raid. Photo by Joan E. Moore, March 2000.

true, it may have resulted in special treatment at the time she was sold to a European and could have mitigated the severity of her experience during the dreaded "Middle Passage" across the Atlantic.[33]

On this, as on so many aspects of the early life of Anna Kingsley, the historical record lacks evidence. Historians of the African diaspora are often forced to make inferences from minimal data, such as the statement by the British commandant Richard Lloyd, mentioned previously, that approximately one thousand captives were available for sale at Gorée Island in 1806. It is presumed here that Anna Kingsley was one of those captives, that she was from Jolof and possibly descended from the royal family, and that she was transported across the Atlantic Ocean in a slave ship and sold as a "bozal" (newly arrived African) by a slave merchant at Havana, Cuba. If anyone subsequently asked about her childhood and the events of her early life, her answers did not survive in written form. There are only the accounts of her as a "royal princess" remembered in legends in Florida and in Senegal.

2 · Havana

Zephaniah Kingsley, Jr.

THE DEMAND FOR Africans was high in Cuba in 1806. Planters had developed huge sugar estates in the rural provinces when exports from Haiti collapsed following the 1789–1803 slave rebellion, which had driven Europeans from that island. Other nations were moving toward abolition of the Atlantic slave trade—Denmark in 1803, England in 1807, and the United States in 1808—but in Cuba the demand for Africans remained insatiable. Ship captains knew the old Cuban saying "sugar is made with blood" contained an element of truth. As long as death rates in sugar production remained high, the slave traders were assured of a profitable market.[1]

It was the promise of profit that brought Captain Francis Ghisolfi and the *Sally* to Havana in July 1806. The *Sally* hailed from the Danish island of St. Thomas in the West Indies, where the port city, Charlotte Amalie, was an important transshipment center in the Atlantic trade. Large ships four to twelve weeks out from Africa stopped at St. Thomas to off-load their human cargoes to smaller vessels for delivery to other ports in the Caribbean. The *Sally* was one of three Danish and three American ships that carried a total of 673 enslaved Africans to Havana in July 1806. Six more ships arrived during August and September with another 587 Africans.[2]

Among the ships that landed in September was the *Esther*, carrying a cargo of 43 male slaves. The ship carried American registration papers, although both the captain, Henry Wright, and the owner, Zephaniah Kingsley, Jr., were citizens of Spanish East Florida. Kingsley, born in Bristol, England, in 1765, was reared in Charleston, South Carolina, where his father, a Quaker, was a successful merchant. In 1782 the elder Kingsley moved his family to Nova Scotia after having been banished from South Carolina for his loyal support of King George III during the American Revolution. Zephaniah, Jr., returned briefly to Charleston in 1793 and then moved to Haiti, St. Thomas, and Spanish East Florida and a life as a maritime merchant, planter, and slave owner. Between 1798 and 1803 Kingsley had been a Danish citizen and, like Ghisolfi, had sailed out of Charlotte Amalie and engaged in the African slave trade. In 1803 Kingsley moved to Florida, where he pledged fidelity to Spain and imported slaves to work a plantation. He also continued in the African trade.

Captain Ghisolfi and the *Sally* had been in Havana several times before, but never with a cargo of more females than males. Normally the ratio was two males to every female, but on this voyage the *Sally* carried 120 Africans, 99 of them women, more than 80 percent. Among the women were 22 teenagers.[3]

It is possible that Anta Majigeen Ndiaye was one of the twenty-two teenagers, although the evidence is only circumstantial. The name of the ship that carried her is listed in Cuban port-of-entry records, along with the name and nationality of the captain in command, and the approximate age and gender of the 1,260 enslaved Africans who arrived at Havana from July through September 1806. Age and gender were recorded, but the personal names of these Africans who entered the Havana port were not. Buyers wanted to know the age, health condition, sex, and sometimes the ethnic identity of the Africans exhibited for sale; names were of little importance to them.

An enormous amount of aggregate data concerning the Atlantic slave trade became available for study in 1999 through the efforts of historians Stephen Behrendt, David Eltis, and David Richardson, who collected data from more than 26,000 slaving voyages across the Atlantic Ocean between 1650 and 1870. The authors estimate that 11 million Africans were forced onto slave ships and carried to ports in the Americas. It was the largest mass migration in human history, and it exacted heavy casualties. Fewer than 9.5 million were alive when the ships arrived in American ports; 15 percent died during the Atlantic crossings. So many ships carried Africans across the Atlantic Ocean between 1500 and 1870 that the term *Middle Passage* has come to symbolize the suffering and death that came to represent one of the most ignominious chapters in human history.[4]

It is thus not possible to ascertain exactly which ship carried a Wolof teenager named Anta into Havana. Analysis of the aggregate data provides answers to vitally important questions about the numbers of Africans who departed the various African ports, percentages of those who died en route, male/female ratios, and the number of weeks required for the ocean passage. Unfortunately, the names of specific individuals cannot be found in the data.

Whatever slave ship transported Anta from Senegal to Cuba, it undoubtedly carried a cargo of Africans who suffered from a variety of ailments. Many who survived the passage arrived in port afflicted by dehydration and dysentery after being confined in the fetid bowels of ships where temperatures sometimes climbed as high as 120 degrees. Captains conserved water supplies by limiting slaves to between one and three pints of water per day, with Liverpool ships generally allowing two pints per slave per day. Relief from the stench of seasickness came only during cool days and brief exercise periods on deck. The dead and dying were generally dumped into the sea during the crossing. Few masters disrupted their ships' routines with ceremonies to recognize the human casualties the slave trade created.[5]

Survivors received perfunctory medical inspections after the ships anchored at American ports, and brief quarantines were enforced when epidemic diseases were detected. During these immobile days crew members prepared the captives for sale, adding fresh vegetables and fruits to their diets and bathing and oiling their skin to make them look healthy for buyer inspections. Buyers were unlikely to pay high prices for newly arrived Africans who appeared ill and weak.

When the quarantine period expired, guards moved the survivors down the gangplanks of the slave ships. The Havana market was the center of commerce for Spain's colonies in the Americas. Crowds of buyers searched for lumber and salt fish from New England, meats and grain from other American states, cloth and manufactured goods from England, and slaves from Africa. Merchants hailed from North America, Europe, the Caribbean islands, and South America. Ships departed daily loaded with sugar, rum, and African slaves.[6]

Anta Majigeen Ndiaye was exhibited for sale in late September or early October 1806. The record is clear that she was purchased by Zephaniah Kingsley, a slave trader and Florida planter. Kingsley had been in Havana since September 18, continuing a slave-trading expedition that had originated at Charleston. Two years earlier, on August 14, 1804, he had sold a 300-ton vessel, the *Gustavia*, to a Charleston merchant, Spencer John Man. With a Captain T. Hill in command and Kingsley aboard as business manager, the vessel was dispatched to Liverpool, England, for overhaul and refitting and an eventual journey to Africa to purchase slaves.[7]

The *Gustavia* sailed from Liverpool to Cape Town, South Africa, and then proceeded to Mozambique on the East African coast. It was back at Charleston April 28, 1806, with 250 enslaved Africans. Five months later Kingsley arrived in Havana on another ship, the *Esther*. The 43 slaves carried aboard were apparently the unsold portion of the Africans previously purchased in East Africa.[8]

Five years later, in 1811, Kingsley testified that he purchased a "black woman called Anna, around eighteen years of age, bought as a bozal in the port of Havana from a slave cargo."[9] In 1835 two men who had been Kingsley's neighbors twenty years before testified that they knew Anna from the day she first arrived at Laurel Grove Plantation in East Florida, late in 1806. The evidence, therefore, points toward a date of purchase between the day Kingsley landed at Havana (September 18) and the day he departed (October 10).[10]

When the *Esther* left Havana for St. Augustine, its customs manifest listed a cargo of four hogsheads of molasses, twenty-eight half-pipes, and twelve whole pipes of rum, all consigned to Charleston merchant Spencer Man. The manifest also listed human cargo: "tres negras bozales," or three black females newly arrived from Africa. During his stay in Havana, Kingsley had purchased them. A thirteen-year-old girl from Jolof named Anta Majigeen Ndiaye was almost certainly one of the three.[11]

On October 24 the *Esther* anchored off the port of St. Augustine while Kingsley rowed ashore to register three new female residents of the province. The following day the *Esther* pulled anchor and sailed north along thirty-five miles of northeast Florida's shoreline to the mouth of the St. Johns River. Captain Wright steered the vessel west and sailed upriver, traveling alongside huge expanses of marsh, occasional fields of corn and cotton, and widely scattered settlements. The most common sight was pine forest, with occasional oak hammocks and stretches of cypress and bay trees. There were no rocky ledges like those Anta had seen at Gorée, only occasional shell mounds forty to fifty feet high covered with tree growth. After passing through a narrows known as the Cowford, a trading center and ferry crossing that would later become the town of Jacksonville, the schooner was tied to a wharf at Laurel Grove Plantation, slightly north of an inlet on the west of the St. Johns River known as Doctors Lake. The *Esther* had sailed forty miles upriver.

Beyond the dock at Laurel Grove, a path led up a slight incline to Kingsley's two-story dwelling house. Visible as well were the wooden houses in the slave quarter, agricultural fields, and citrus groves. Once again Anta walked down a ship's gangplank, this time to step ashore at Laurel Grove, her new home in the Americas. Her place of residence would not be in the slave quarters, however. Instead she was taken directly to Kingsley's dwelling house. Anta had celebrated only thirteen birthdays, and already she was pregnant with his child.

In July 1842, almost forty years after Anna Madgigine Jai landed at Laurel Grove Plantation, Zephaniah Kingsley was interviewed in New York City by the abolitionist Lydia Maria Child. She asked him, "Where did you become acquainted with your wife?" Child remembered that Kingsley replied, in one of many remarks that led her to characterize him as "altogether unaccountable," "On the coast of Africa, Ma'am. She was a new nigger, when I first saw her."[12] One year later, Kingsley wrote in his will that he and Anna were married "in a foreign land" where the ceremony was "celebrated and solemnized by her native African custom, altho' never celebrated according to the forms of Christian usage."[13]

These two remarks have been combined and used as evidence that Anna was an African princess married to Kingsley in a ceremony on the African coast. One oral legend the author heard in the mid-1970s conjured a scene set on the African coast, wherein Anna's father, an African king, gave her away in marriage to Kingsley. The implication was that the two men were partners in the slave trade.[14]

While there is circumstantial evidence to support the legend of Anna descending from a royal family, there is nothing credible to document that Kingsley first saw her on the African coast or that they were married in Africa. The evidence points instead to a more mundane conclusion. Kingsley gave testimony to a Spanish official in 1811 that he purchased Anna "as a bozal in the port of Havana from a slave cargo."[15] In his 1843 will, Kingsley says he and Anna were married in a "foreign land"; he does not specify Africa. Nor does his comment that the wedding was sanctified by "African custom" constitute proof that it took place in Africa. Furthermore, the term "new nigger" was used in the Americas to describe slaves "newly arrived" from Africa who were unfamiliar with the prevailing languages and customs. "New nigger" and "bozal" were interchangeable terms. A slave trader with years of experience purchasing slaves in Africa and selling and owning them in the Americas would not call an African in Africa a "new nigger."

The "foreign land" where the "native African custom" that constituted their wedding occurred was undoubtedly Cuba. It is probable that Lydia Maria Child's memory was inaccurate concerning Kingsley's response to the query "Where did you become acquainted with your wife?" He would more likely have said *from*, rather than *on*, the coast of Africa.[16]

For the remaining thirty-seven years of his life, Kingsley referred to Anta as his wife. He called her Anna and lived openly with her and their mixed-race children. After nearly forty years together, Kingsley described Anna as "a fine, tall figure, black as jet, but very handsome.

She was very capable, and could carry on all the affairs of the plantation in my absence, as well as I could myself. She was affectionate and faithful, and I could trust her."[17]

In the Americas, Anta would be known as Anna Madgigine Jai Kingsley, reflecting the way her African names were transcribed into Spanish and English by officials in Florida. She would alternately refer to herself as Anna Kingsley, Anna Madgigine, and Anna Jai. The Spanish and American officials who heard the unfamiliar African names recorded them in diverse ways, but it is clear that Anna intended to perpetuate the names of her parents in Florida. Penda Mbow, a scholar in Senegal who is familiar with the history of Anna Kingsley, has stated that she exemplifies the pride and adaptability that were the norm among Wolof women of the African diaspora.[18]

3 · Laurel Grove

Anna Madgigine Jai Kingsley

GIVEN THE TRAUMATIC EVENTS of her thirteenth year, Anna Madgigine Jai Kingsley had little choice but to mature rapidly. At an age when Wolof girls were only beginning to put aside childhood games to learn the first lessons of womanhood from their mothers, Anna had been torn from family and homeland and sold across the ocean as a slave. Still in her thirteenth year, she had been purchased in Havana and made pregnant by a white plantation owner from Florida. In the months before the birth of her first child, Anna became the manager of Kingsley's household at Laurel Grove.[1]

Anna's adjustment to life at Laurel Grove was perhaps made easier by the ways in which it reminded her of Jolof. With the exception of occasional craftsmen hired to work at the shipyards, nearly everyone was from Africa. Enslaved men and women of Ibo, Susu, and Calabari ethnicity worked the cotton fields and performed skilled labor in the carpentry and black-smith shops, just as enslaved Bambara, Fula, and Sereer peoples had cultivated millet and woven cloth in Wolof villages. The more than one hundred workers living in rows of wooden houses at the slave quarters came from several West and East African nations. The languages of Kamba, Calabari, Susu, Baga, Wolof, Ibo, and other African peoples might be heard on any given day. The

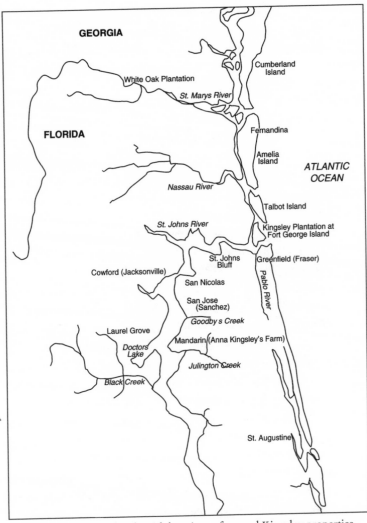

Map 2. Northeast Florida with locations of several Kingsley properties, including Anna Kingsley's farm at today's Mandarin, ca. 1810–1821.

workers came from diverse cultural and religious backgrounds, yet they worked and lived together amicably and were creating a medium of communication and a creole culture. Names like Bonafy, Qualla, Abdalla, Bella, Tamassa, Comba, Coonta, Tamba, Penda, Nassebo, Yamba, Jenoma, McGuindo, Cabo Mouse, and M'toto were called out daily. At Laurel Grove, Anna found a transplanted African village inhabited by black men and women from distant nations and cultures.[2]

Two of the field laborers, Jacob and Camilla, lived in the village with their son Jim. Jacob was an Ibo from what is today known as Nigeria; Camilla was from Rio Pongo on the coast of the modern Republic of Guinea, probably of Susu ethnicity. Jim was born at Laurel Grove. Jack, one of the plantation carpenters, and Tamassa were from East Africa, and were the parents of four children: Ben, Molly, Rose, and M'toto (the Swahili word for child), all born at Laurel Grove.[3]

Zephaniah Kingsley's slave families were housed in separate quarters at Laurel Grove and at two nearby subdivisions called Shipyard and Springfield. At each location were found dwelling houses, slave quarters, poultry coops, cart houses, carpentry shops, mill houses, corn and pea cribs, and barns for cotton gins, bales of cotton, horses, and mules. At Laurel Grove a citrus grove of 760 mandarin orange trees was surrounded by a picket fence and a two-thousand-foot hedge of bearing orange trees. On sandy soils nearby were two hundred acres of cleared land planted in Sea Island cotton. Sugarcane grew in fields on the north shore of Doctors Lake. Kingsley also maintained several large fields of potatoes, corn, and beans to feed his workers throughout the year. Surplus provisions were sold at market. Each family was assigned a separate dwelling and a plot of land for its own corn and vegetable gardens.

Abraham Hannahan was general manager of Laurel Grove. A slave of mixed-race ancestry born and reared at Charleston in the household of Kingsley's father, Hannahan was brought to East Florida in 1804 and placed in charge of Laurel Grove. There he directed trusted slave "drivers" who assigned each day's tasks to the enslaved laborers and watched to see that the work was completed satisfactorily. An African named Peter was in charge at Springfield, and was second in command under Hannahan. Kingsley called Peter a mechanic and valuable manager worth at least a $1,000 in 1812. African men and women left their quarters at sunrise to work at assigned tasks in the fields or forests until approximately two o'clock each afternoon. When tasks were completed, workers were able to organize their personal time for hunting, fishing, and recreation, or for cultivating their own vegetable gardens and tending to their poultry and small livestock.[4]

This was a pattern of labor readily recognizable to Anna, whose uncles had sent slaves to labor in the millet fields of Jolof. Under Peter's direction the workers at the Springfield settlement produced eight hundred bushels of corn and four hundred bushels of field peas in a year, in addition to caring for poultry, hogs, and cattle. Peter was in charge of a mill house where corn and other grains were ground into flour.

Only a small portion of Laurel Grove had been cleared when Anna first arrived there. Reserves of pine forests and wetlands were available for future expansion. Although the soil types, vegetation, and levels of precipitation at Laurel Grove differed greatly from conditions with which she was familiar in Jolof, Anna would have noticed similarities between the reserve lands Kingsley owned and the shifting cultivation patterns of Senegal, where crops and entire villages were moved onto idle, brush-covered land when soil fertility in the millet fields diminished. The size and complexity of Kingsley's operation must have surprised Anna. In addition to the planting activities and the shipyard and cotton gins, he kept a retail store stocked with tools and other items for trade with families and planters in the surrounding area. Kingsley's enterprise was more elaborate than any of the slave villages Anna would have seen in Jolof.

One of the African women transported with Anna from Gorée to Havana, and later from Havana to East Florida aboard the *Esther*, is also believed to have come from Jolof. Through these experiences, Anna and Sophie Chidgigine formed bonds that functioned as a kinship tie in later years. The two Jolof women were able to converse in the Wolof language they shared from their homeland. Sophie became the wife of Abraham Hannahan. Zephaniah later freed Abraham and Sophie and their children; the lives of the two families would remain intertwined for decades.[5]

In the months after her arrival at Laurel Grove, Anna would have heard of other African women who were the wives or mistresses of white plantation owners. Molly Erwin was the wife of James Erwin, who worked fifty slaves on his rice plantation on the St. Marys River. The two black wives and children of George J. F. Clarke, an important official with the Spanish government of East Florida, were well known in the area. Francisco Xavier Sánchez and several other prominent Florida men had black or mixed-race wives or mistresses and raised their interracial children in familial bonds. Only the interracial nature of these unions would have been outside Anna's experiences in Jolof. A familiar route to freedom for slave women in Wolof villages was marriage to their owners or other freeborn men in the compounds and giving birth to their children.[6]

For example, John Fraser, a Scots-born ship captain, was married to Phenda, an African woman from Rio Pongo on the Guinea Coast. At Bangalan, the farthest navigable point up the Pongo, Fraser maintained a fortified holding pen for slaves he purchased from convoys captured in wars and slave raids in the interior and marched to Bangalan along paths that reached as far as the Futa Jalon region of Guinea. Fraser then sent the Africans to slave markets in the Americas aboard his own ships. He eventually established a residence and business at Charleston, bringing his son with him while his wife and daughters remained in Africa. In 1809, the year after the United States outlawed slave importations, Fraser moved to Spanish East Florida, where the slave trade was still legal. He purchased two estates, a cotton plantation on the St. Johns River and a rice plantation on the St. Marys River, and brought 370 enslaved Africans to cultivate them.[7]

Francis Richard, Jr., moved to East Florida from St. Domingue to escape the slave rebellion that eventually drove the French from the island and led to the establishment of the independent nation of Haiti. Richard had a white family and legitimate heirs. He also fathered mixed-race children by two slave women whom he freed and acknowledged as his consorts and eventually relocated in Haiti. His will recognized his mixed-race and white children and provided them all with considerable property. Richard's "colored" children were educated property owners and substantial citizens of East Florida for decades. Richard's daughter, Cornelia, married a white planter named John Taylor and managed a large estate after her husband's death. Richard's son Fortune owned a 370-acre plantation on Little Pottsburgh Creek. Another son, John, was a successful blacksmith in Jacksonville until 1862, when he joined the U.S. Colored Infantry and fought for the Union during the Civil War. Anna Kingsley's family and the Richard family interacted for at least three generations, in Florida and in Haiti.[8]

Men like Fraser, Kingsley, Clarke, and Richard saw in Florida's climate, soil, and waterways the opportunity for great wealth, but only if they could acquire sufficient numbers of slaves to do the necessary agricultural work. Yet they felt race did not automatically and permanently consign persons of color to slavery. According to Kingsley, "color ought not be the badge of degradation"; the only distinction should be between slave and free, not between white and colored.[9]

Kingsley justified enslaving Africans by claiming they were better suited to work in the hot Florida sun than their pale European counterparts. "Nature," he wrote, "has not fitted a white complexion for hard work in the sun, as it is evident that the darkness of complexion here is a measure of capacity for endurance of labor."[10] In Kingsley's opinion, whites had two alternatives in Florida: either abandon the land or make use of large numbers of black slaves.

Kingsley chose to employ black slaves, but with this decision came the possibility that his laborers might run away or violently reject their bondage. He advocated humane treatment and encouraged slaves to live in family units and perpetuate their African customs. But more was needed to ensure the personal safety of the white patriarchs. Kingsley called for liberal manumission laws and policies that could convince "the free colored population to be attached to good order and have a friendly feeling towards the white population."[11] Men like Abraham Hannahan, who had talent and leadership ability, should be freed and given personal property rights and encouraged to join with white slave owners. Once united, whites and free blacks would be able to control the much larger group of enslaved blacks whose labor created the riches that justified the overall system. Kingsley freed Hannahan in 1811.[12]

The relationship between Anna and Zephaniah was open and familial and would continue so for nearly forty years. While Kingsley acknowledged Anna as his wife and praised her character and virtue, he also had other slave concubines who gave birth to his children. Anna was the senior figure, carrying the authority of the recognized first wife in a polygamous household whose customs were observed by all in the Kingsley extended family even if they were outside the legal bounds of marriage in either Spanish or American society. Reared in Africa in a polygamous family, Anna would have been familiar with co-wife relationships, tolerant of them, and cooperative with the other wives.

The white men and women who visited Laurel Grove were not always aware of Kingsley's other women. Those who met Anna when she first arrived in Florida recognized her special relationship with Zephaniah and concluded that she was a free woman. John M. Bowden testified in the 1830s that he had known Anna "from the time she first came into the country and she was always called and considered a free person of color."[13] And yet for the first four years she was in America, Anna was legally a slave and Kingsley was thirty years her senior, engaged in a dangerous life as ship captain and slave plantation owner. Had his ship gone down during one of his Caribbean voyages, Anna would have appeared on a subsequent property inventory, and she and her children would have been sold at auction.

Kingsley once commented that he was unsure how his marriage to Anna would be considered under the law. They had been married, he said, "in a foreign land" where the ceremony was "celebrated and solemnized by her native African custom, altho' never celebrated according to the forms of Christian usage." But there was never any doubt about her status: "She has always been respected as my wife and as such I acknowledge her, nor do I think that her truth, honor, integrity, moral conduct or good sense will lose in comparison with anyone."[14]

Kingsley formally emancipated Anna on March 4, 1811. He wrote, "Let it be known that I . . . possessed as a slave a black woman called Anna, around eighteen years of age, bought as a bozal in the port of Havana from a slave cargo, who with the permission of the government was introduced here; the said black woman has given birth to three mulatto children: George, about 3 years 9 months, Martha, 20 months old, and Mary, one month old. And regarding the good qualities shown by the said black woman, the nicety and fidelity which she has shown me, and for other reasons, I have resolved to set her free . . . and the same to her three children."[15]

After almost five years of enslavement, Anna Kingsley was again a free woman. Three children would share her freedom. At first, Anna remained at Laurel Grove as the wife of Zephaniah Kingsley and manager of his household. She would also help manage the plantation in her husband's absence.

Abraham Hannahan, emancipated only days after Anna, continued on as plantation manager. Given land at Laurel Grove, Hannahan built a house and barn and expanded his responsibilities by assuming some of the duties for Kingsley's store. During Abraham's travels on the St. Johns River selling goods to farmers and to Seminole Indians, Anna assumed more responsibilities at Laurel Grove. Kingsley later said her managerial abilities rivaled his own.[16]

Responsible management at Laurel Grove was greatly needed as Kingsley was seldom in residence. For years he relied on slaves to manage his property while he sailed in the West Indies trade. During the years 1802–17 he hired several captains to keep his ships in regular service to ports in Cuba, Puerto Rico, St. Thomas, and Jamaica in the West Indies, and to Natchez, Savannah, Charleston, Wilmington, New York, and Fernandina. When Kingsley was in command, he sailed with an all-black crew. Even his sailors were slaves.

By 1811 Zephaniah Kingsley was a rich man. In addition to Laurel Grove, he owned Drayton Island, a large plantation at Lake George on the St. Johns River; White Oak Plantation on the St. Marys River, a large and highly profitable rice plantation; and several other properties. Plantations and milling operations experienced unprecedented prosperity in the first decade of the nineteenth century. Kingsley's shipping and mercantile operations were prospering. Given Kingsley's affluence, it is unlikely that lack of material comforts would have led Anna to make significant changes in her life. And yet in 1812, the year after she achieved emancipation, Anna Kingsley moved away from Laurel Grove.

4 · The Patriot War

THROUGHOUT her adult years Anna proved to be an independent and capable woman, concerned about business investments and actively involved in managing her family's financial affairs. Perhaps it was this independent nature that prompted her to strike out on her own. She would continue her relationship with Zephaniah Kingsley until his death in 1843, but in 1812, one year after gaining freedom for herself and her children, Anna moved across the St. Johns River and established a homestead on five acres granted to her by the Spanish government.

Anna's property was located directly across from Laurel Grove on the eastern shore of the St. Johns River, near a twenty-acre tract known as the "Horse Landing." Today the site is near County Dock Road in Old Mandarin. Anna's property was bounded on the south by the 1,250-acre property of Alexander Creighton, and on the north by 100 acres known as "Sharon" that John and Susan Faulk owned in 1813. The "Horse Landing" adjoined the Faulk property. St. Anthony's Point, granted to Uriah Bowden and inherited by his son, Moses Bowden, was located at the northern boundary of the Faulk homestead. In the 1770s, when East Florida was a British province and the American Revolution was under way, Loyalist refugees had established several small farms in an undeveloped portion of Francis Levett's 10,000-acre Julianton Plantation.

In 1813 several of Anna's neighbors were descendants of these Loyalist families.[1]

Why Anna moved to this location is not stated in the historical record. A five-acre farm would not have been sufficient to support a household of three children and twelve slaves. The location was convenient for travel to Laurel Grove, where Anna continued to exercise management during her husband's many absences.

One possible explanation is that a site near the landing was chosen to expand Zephaniah's mercantile operations to farms across the St. Johns River. Kingsley's retail store at Laurel Grove, located on the first floor of his dwelling house, had become a success by 1812. He expanded his retail business by outfitting boats with trade goods and sending them up the St. Johns River to peddle wares to farmers and Seminole Indians. Farmers on the east side of the river were potential buyers for the goods Kingsley was importing. The location of Anna's homestead at "Horse Landing" was convenient for boat traffic to and from the expanding small farms and plantations on the east shore of the St. Johns. A road that terminated at the landing facilitated transport of merchandise to homesteads located away from the river on roads leading to the Cowford (now Jacksonville) and St. Augustine. It is worth noting that the design of Anna's building resembled the combination dwelling and retail store that Zephaniah built for himself at Laurel Grove. Both dwellings were constructed in 1812.[2]

Zephaniah sent slave carpenters from Laurel Grove to build Anna's residence. John M. Bowden later described the dwelling as measuring thirty feet square, a "large and comfortable house" of stone on the first floor, hewn logs on the second, with a shingle roof, and constructed in the fashion of a block house.[3] Bowden said the home was well finished and worth between $500 and $600. As in Zephaniah's dwelling at Laurel Grove, the lower floor stored grain, nails, spikes, chains, axes, and general farming tools. Anna and her three children lived in the comfortably furnished second story of the building.

In the compound outside the family dwelling were farm animals, cleared fields, and a poultry yard that drew praise from neighbors. John M. Bowden said he "did not know another poultry yard in the country equal to that of [Anna Kingsley]. She had a great many large

English ducks."[4] Anna said she had ten dozen ducks and four dozen chickens in November 1813.

In addition to the home built for Anna and her family, carpenters constructed houses for Anna's slaves. Although a former slave herself, Anna became the owner of twelve slaves after her own emancipation: two men, three women, and seven children. Her roots were in an African society where slavery had been integral to the social fabric for centuries; it was there that her conceptions of social relationships were formed. Anna Kingsley would own slaves as late as 1860.

Anna's Florida neighbors would not have thought it unusual that she owned slaves. Spanish law viewed slaves as persons created by God and endowed with a soul and a moral personality, the unfortunate victims of fate or war. They had rights under Spanish law that were enforced by the courts, including the sanctity of marriage, the right to be freed for meritorious acts, and the right of self-purchase. They were also permitted to work at extra jobs in order to earn the money to purchase their own freedom. The unfree status of Spanish slaves was neither preordained nor permanent; and once freed, they were entitled to own property, including human property.[5]

Free blacks could be found working in St. Augustine as skilled craftsmen and wage laborers. Some were homeowners; several owned farms and slaves outside of St. Augustine. Over the years free black militia companies provided invaluable defense for the province. The historian Jane Landers has painstakingly searched the Spanish records to reconstruct the story of the free black community and militia of East Florida. Her work has restored black men and women like Francisco Menéndez and Prince and Judy Witten to their rightful place of importance in Florida history. Among the many dynamic persons about whom Landers has written is Jorge Biassou, commander of an army of 40,000 men during the slave rebellion in St. Domingue. Even François Dominique Touissant-L'Ouverture, the Haitian liberator, had been his subordinate. Biassou joined forces with the Spanish of Hispaniola and was sent to East Florida after Spain and France agreed to peace terms in 1795. In his new East Florida home, Biassou was placed in command of the free black militia. He and his large family provided invaluable services to Spain on the East Florida frontier.[6]

It was not unusual for the Spanish colonial government to recognize Anna Kingsley's freedom, nor to grant her land and permit her to own slaves. Racial prejudice existed in Spanish East Florida, but it lacked the exclusionary rigidity found in nearby Georgia and South Carolina. Manumission was encouraged, and, once freed, black women and men were able to participate in the Spanish colonial system through baptism, marriage, land grants, litigation, and kinship networks. Plagued with frequent invasions and internal rebellions, and hampered by inferior military forces, East Florida's governors depended on free black militia units and Indian allies to retain control of the province. The geopolitical situation thus worked to keep a relaxed racial system in place in Spanish East Florida while it was vanishing in nearby Spanish Cuba.[7]

As a free black woman in a frontier society, Anna was entitled to specific rights and privileges recognized in medieval Spanish law. She could hold property, manage plantations, testify and litigate in the courts, and engage in business activities. She became a Catholic during her stay on the St. Johns River, probably converted by a Spanish priest during an annual visit to bring the sacraments to residents of the rural settlements. She later utilized the Catholic Church to protect her rights and bind her family to powerful patrons, forming extended kinship networks through godparent ties. Fictive kinship networks linked by mutual obligations were significant in Hispanic communities, as they had been in her village in Jolof. Anna would use these kinship ties for her own children and grandchildren, even after Florida became an American territory.[8]

If dignity and independence are words that describe Anna's character, then tragedy, adaptability, and perseverance characterize her life. While Anna supervised her slaves as they established a successful farmstead, an invasion of East Florida was being planned that would threaten all she had achieved, including her freedom. Land-hungry Georgians and Carolinians plotted with dissident Spanish subjects to foment rebellion and attach Florida to the United States. Beset by troubles at home and rebellion in its South American colonies, Spain was unable to govern Florida effectively.

In 1812, the same year Anna established her own estate, the Patriot Rebellion began. Instigated and financed covertly by the President of the United States, James Madison, and his Secretary of State, James Monroe, and supported by American soldiers and sailors who crossed East Florida's northern border as advisors to the insurgents, the "Patriots" took the town of Fernandina and moved south to control the St. Johns River and begin a siege outside St. Augustine.[9]

Zephaniah Kingsley was abducted in the first days of the invasion and held hostage until he signed a pledge of support for the rebels. His fortified buildings at Laurel Grove were seized by the invaders and used as their headquarters for raids on Indian villages in Alachua. Although he would later deny it, Kingsley became a supporter of the insurgency.[10]

The main Patriot invading force at the time camped outside St. Augustine under the joint command of John H. McIntosh and officers of the U.S. Army. In July 1812, after realizing he would have to surrender St. Augustine if food supplies could not be found for the town's residents, Governor Sebastián Kindelán ordered his Seminole allies to attack the outlying settlements along the St. Johns and St. Marys Rivers. The governor predicted the attacks would force many of the rebels to abandon the siege lines and return home to defend their families and property. The strategy worked, although it devastated the previously thriving plantations.

For Zephaniah Kingsley the attack meant the destruction of most of Laurel Grove and the loss of forty-one Africans to the Seminole raiders. The Seminoles of Alachua had previously traded amicably with Kingsley, but their warriors would not spare the headquarters from which raids on their villages were being staged. The only building remaining at Laurel Grove after the Seminole raid was the combination dwelling and retail store, which Kingsley had surrounded by a stockade fence and fortified with brass cannons.

Led by the U.S. troops who had covertly directed the insurgency, the Patriots withdrew from St. Augustine to headquarters at Camp New Hope at Goodby's Creek and the St. Johns River. They remained there only briefly, then evacuated the province, destroying plantations as they departed. Not all of the invaders left, however. A number of criminally inclined men had joined the ranks of the Patriots during the invasion, hoping to profit from lawless conditions. When the more principled Patriot leaders and U.S. forces withdrew, the criminals remained in camps along the St. Johns and St. Marys Rivers. Widespread looting and burning followed as the Patriot insurgency degenerated into guerrilla warfare, slave stealing, and border marauding.

Laurel Grove became the headquarters for one of these marauding bands. Kingsley had fled the area by then, his whereabouts as mysterious as his relationsip to the Patriot invaders. In his absence the fortified strong house at Laurel Grove provided the bandits with protection.

. Located in the center of this zone of violence, Anna had more to fear than destruction of her property: If she and her family were captured, they would be driven to Georgia and sold as slaves. Numerous slaves and free blacks had shared that fate during the previous months of fighting. To be captured and enslaved again, this time sharing that fate with her children, must have been unthinkable to Anna. The Spanish gunboats that patrolled along the St. Johns River were her main source of safety. In the event of an attack by the rebels, she might flee with her family to the woods and swamps, a perilous venture given the ages of her children, or seek shelter on the Spanish gunboats.

That attack came in November 1813, led by Colonel Samuel Alexander, a notorious bandit from Georgia. Crewmen on the Spanish gunboats tracked the rebels as they plundered farms along the river. Commander José Antonio Moreno was on patrol aboard the gunboat *Inmutable* on November 21, 1813. Early that morning Moreno departed the Spanish fortification of San Nicolas, located on the south bank of the St. Johns River adjacent to the public ferry crossing known as the Cowford. His orders were to sail to Kingsley Point at the St. Johns River and Doctors Lake, where Kingsley's fortified dwelling house was still in the hands of insurgents. (It was surrounded by a sturdy, seven-foot post-and-clapboard cedar fence, with two four-pounder brass cannons pointing out at the river.)[11]

At daybreak on November 22, the *Inmutable* and the gunboat *Havanera*, under the command of Don Lorenzo Ávila, anchored opposite the fortified house. "Right away with the clear of daylight," Moreno reported, "they opened fire upon us with one of the cannons they have therein, to which we both responded."[12] The insurgents were able to direct effective volleys, but eventually the superior fire-power from the twenty-four-pounder cannons aboard the gunboats "wrecked the whole front of the house although they [the rebels] stayed firm, protecting themselves therein; [whereupon] we fired upon them with grapeshot, and they no longer were shouting and challenging."

After he was sure the rebels had fled to the woods, Moreno pulled anchor and sailed to the eastern shore. There he consulted with a squadron of Spanish troops who were searching for cattle thieves raiding farms in the vicinity of Anna Kingsley's homestead. Their officer informed Moreno that the "rebels appeared to have gone to the other side and taken many cattle."

Moreno's attention was drawn to the western shore, where he saw a canoe enter the St. Johns River from the dock at Laurel Grove. When the canoe came within voice range of the *Inmutable,* the two passengers shouted a password and were permitted to board. Moreno was surprised to discover that one of the canoeists was "the free black woman Ana Kingsley," who boarded the vessel to deliver a letter addressed to Don Tomás Llorente, commandant of the fortification at San Nicolás. The letter came from Roman Sánchez, Patriot leader and a descendant of one of Spanish East Florida's most prominent families.

After receiving assurance from Moreno that her children and slaves would be safe aboard the gunboat, Anna and one of her male slaves pushed the canoe away and paddled back to the western shore. "Shortly afterwards she returned with . . . three small children . . . two male blacks and three mature female blacks with seven children (also small) . . . whom she had hidden in the forest." These were apparently the slaves she owned. She also brought back a number of Kingsley's slaves whom "she had saved from the rebels."

Anna told Moreno that seventy men had been at Laurel Grove when cannon fire from the gunboats prompted them to flee to the woods. Their rifles were left behind during the hasty departure, but when they realized the only casualty had been a horse, they came back to retrieve their weapons and return to hiding places in the woods. The house had been damaged by the gunboats' shells, Anna warned, but the cannons remained in place and were still functional.

Anna then volunteered to lead a party of Spanish soldiers to the abandoned house to confiscate the cannons and bring them to the gunboat. As a token of her fidelity, she left "her children and the slaves as hostages." Twenty free black and mulatto soldiers of the Battalion of Havana, under command of First Sergeant Jorge Arrieta, followed Anna's canoe to the dock at Laurel Grove. Before they could carry out their mission, however, the lookout on the masthead of the *Inmutable* spotted rebel patrols clandestinely infiltrating the woods near the house. Moreno, convinced that Anna had deceived him and lured his men into an ambush, ordered his lookout to signal the men to return to the gunboats.

When she returned, Anna insisted that she had not planned an ambush and accused Sánchez of deceiving her with a false letter for Llorente, and of falsely stating that he and his allies were planning to withdraw from the area.[13] Later that day, Anna volunteered to lead another excursion to the Kingsley house and search the nearby woods for enslaved Africans who might have escaped the rebels. She startled Moreno with a dramatic offer "to set [a] fire so that the house would burn and the rebels would not have this sanctuary." When Moreno consented, Anna departed in a canoe paddled by two black men. Again the craft was tied to the wharf at Laurel Grove. The Spanish commander recorded the return of the party at "seven o'clock" that evening; not a trace of smoke could be seen rising from the buildings. He questioned Anna: "You went to set a fire, and you haven't done anything?" "Wait a moment," was her reply.

Moreno scanned the shoreline with growing skepticism. After a few moments, "a flare came out which grew and reduced the house to ashes, the cannons firing off by themselves when [the fire] reached them." Somehow, Anna had sneaked into the house and "left the fire lit in a trunk full of combustibles so that it would give her time to move away, and the enemies, if they were thereabouts would not come and catch her." The rebels had been completely surprised by the ruse and were "unable to do anything to prevent the fire." Moreno reported that Anna was "greatly pleased to see that the Spaniards' adversaries had nowhere to take refuge and be protected with the artillery." She said "her master would be very content with this as soon as he knew the reasons there were for carrying it out."

This commander did not again doubt Anna's honesty or question her courage. When she asked him to cross to the east side of the St. Johns River where her homestead was located, he immediately gave the order to hoist anchor, noting "her master Kingsley had recently made for her [a home] on a small plot that the government had conceded her." Once her canoe was secured to the dock, Anna moved quickly to the dwelling house. Moreno later reported, "As soon as she was in[side] she brought out a little corn and two rifles and set fire to the house [and] a considerable amount of corn that was inside." Anna told Moreno she had taken this drastic action "so that the rebels would not avail themselves of it, and that it was more gratifying to lose it than that the enemies should take advantage."

When Anna returned to the gunboat after torching her home and the dwelling houses of her slaves, it was late in the evening of November 22. Commander Moreno and his crew had been pursuing the rebels since daybreak, yet he gave orders to his crew to sail the *Inmutable* down river for the safety of the Spanish fortification at San Nicolás. In his official report Moreno wrote about Anna Kingsley, "[I] cannot help but recommend this woman, who has demonstrated a great enthusiasm concerning the Spaniards and extreme aversion to the rebels, being worthy of being looked after, since she has worked like a heroine, destroying the strong house with the fire she set so that the artillery could not be obtained, and later doing the same with her own property."

Tomás Llorente, commander at San Nicolás, wrote to the governor, "Anna M. Kingsley deserves any favor the governor can grant her. Rather than afford shelter and provisions to the enemies of His Majesty . . . [she] burned it all up and remained unsheltered from the weather; the royal order provides rewards for such services."[14] Anna would later receive a 350-acre land grant as compensation for her losses and for her heroic defense of the province.

Although she was only twenty years old at the time, Anna Kingsley had been through crises like this before in her native Jolof. During her first thirteen years, tyeddo raiders from Kajoor had repeatedly pillaged and torched family compounds in Wolof villages in Jolof; the residents were either captured and enslaved or forced to flee. Anna had been one of the captives, had survived the ordeal of an ocean crossing, and had been resettled on the St. Johns River. For a short time her life had been tranquil, until Samuel Alexander and his marauding band from Georgia pillaged and torched East Florida settlements and captured slave and free blacks, marching them north to sell at slave markets in Georgia. Little of substance differentiated the tyeddo raiders from Kajoor and Alexander's marauders from Georgia.

In December 1813, Zephaniah joined Anna at San Nicolás. One month later the Kingsley family boarded a schooner and sailed to Fernandina, followed by a flotilla of rafts loaded with property salvaged from the ruins at Laurel Grove and the slaves who remained after the Indian raid and Patriot depredations. The Kingsleys lived at Fernandina under protection of a Spanish garrison until the outlying plantations were secure from marauders.

5 · Fort George Island

EARLY IN MARCH 1814, Anna and Zephaniah Kingsley sailed from Fernandina to Fort George Island, accompanied by their children, George, Martha, and Mary. Also aboard the ship were slave laborers and the tools, supplies, and equipment needed for a major rebuilding project. At first the emphasis would be on restoring the barrier-island plantation to its former prosperity. Eventually, a new home for Anna would be built close to the dwelling Zephaniah occupied. She would live in the "Ma'am Anna House" until 1838, rear her children in safety, and experience the only prolonged period of peace and stability during her lifetime.

Kingsley had previously arranged to lease the plantation for two years, with an option to purchase. The owner, John H. McIntosh, the leader of the Patriot Rebellion, had fled across the St. Marys River to Georgia to escape the wrath of Spanish officials. Bands of marauders still plagued outlying estates, but Kingsley apparently felt the plantation's island location at the mouth of the St. Johns River provided adequate security.[1]

The vessel sailed south from Fernandina on the inland waterway west of Amelia Island, crossed Nassau Sound, and continued along the western shore of Big Talbot Island. The view along the way was anything but peaceful. Visible on the shores were plantation buildings damaged by the "Patriots" as they withdrew from East Florida. Only two homesteads could be seen on Talbot, with citrus groves and buildings showing the destruction left by the departed insurgents. From the Georgia border to St. Augustine and for seventy miles beyond, as far south as New Smyrna, plantations lay in ruins. In the aftermath of the insurgency, East Florida's planters were desperate to acquire slaves to replace those stolen by the invaders, and to restore dwellings and agricultural fields.[2]

Once the ship passed the southern point of Talbot Island, the view across the inlet encompassed vast fields of marsh grass extending into the waterway from both Talbot and Fort George Islands. Where the marsh touched the shorelines, large trees with overhanging limbs of deep green foliage reached to the water's edge. Looming ahead was a large, two-story white house with a deck on the rooftop overlooking the Atlantic Ocean to the east and a long walkway leading to a wharf on Fort George Inlet. Cooling green vegetation and placid waters belied the violence that had occurred at the island in the preceding years.

Once the ship was secured to the wharf and the occupants had inspected the owner's complex, the damage inflicted during the Patriot insurgency became evident. The main dwelling had been vandalized and looted (even the locks on the doors had been stolen), and it was the only structure left standing on the island. Wooden buildings that had once housed more than 200 slaves were charred ruins. Dwellings for overseers and outbuildings that had sheltered farm animals and implements no longer existed.[3]

Hard work by the carpenters restored the house to a livable condition in short order. Built in 1791 on a foundation of coquina blocks, the wood-frame house had a first story that expanded outward from a rectangular "great room" with fireplaces at the east and west walls. Attached porches on the north and south led to bedrooms at each of the four corners. An outside stairway ascended from the porch on the south to bedrooms on the second floor and to an attic above, where a trapdoor opened to the observation deck.[4]

Construction of temporary slave quarters began immediately. Palmetto fronds were probably gathered on the island to fashion African-style dwellings with thatch roofs. After these were completed, Kingsley sent his laborers into the weed-filled fields to prepare them for planting. Two months later they began planting corn, beans, potatoes, and cotton. Planting activities were behind schedule in 1814, having been delayed by the interlude at Fernandina and the shortage of hands after the 1812 attacks on Laurel Grove. The cotton and provisions fields were eventually restored to profitability, and citrus groves and cane fields were planted.[5]

The same management system was installed at Fort George Island that had proved successful at Laurel Grove Plantation. The "task" system was again used, whereby drivers gave the laborers work assignments sufficient to occupy them from dawn until mid-afternoon on Monday through Friday and until noon on Saturday. After completing their tasks, the men and women were at liberty to work in their own gardens or to fish or hunt to supplement the weekly provisions supplied by the owners. They could also work for hire and keep the money they earned. Enslaved laborers were permitted to purchase freedom for half their assessed price.[6]

The only breaks from this routine came in observance of three holidays. Special foods and extra rations were provided at Christmas, and the slaves were allowed to entertain visitors. There was also a spring holiday, when the workers planted corn and other vegetables in their personal gardens. Another holiday in early October coincided with the harvest of their crops. Life in the slave quarters was family-based, a system intended in part as a social-control measure.

Anna Kingsley was a partner in the planting process at Fort George Island. She inspected the health of the workers each day, nursed illnesses and injuries, and once again filled in as manager during Kingsley's absences. In addition, she continued as Kingsley's household manager, supervising food preparation and other domestic activities. She also directed the labors of her own slaves, who were quartered with the other workers.[7]

It is not known when the dwelling that came to be known as the "Ma'am Anna House" was constructed. Anna and her children did not stay continuously at Fort George Island in the beginning. Antonio Álvarez saw her often at Amelia Island during that year, noting that "she used to come and go between Amelia and Fort George, where she part of the time resided."[8] Zephaniah kept a residence and a wharf at Fernandina, the best deep-water port in East Florida, where the import of enslaved Africans was still a major commercial enterprise. In 1815 Anna also resided occasionally at a residence at San Pablo Plantation, on the St. Johns River, across from Fort George Island.

The decade of the 1820s, after the United States acquired Florida from Spain, is most probably when the "Ma'am Anna House" was built. Zephaniah's relatives began visiting Fort George Island on a regular basis during that decade. His sister and brother-in-law, Isabella and George Gibbs, became Florida residents and lived temporarily at Fort George Island. By 1830 two of their sons (Kingsley Beatty and Zephaniah C. Gibbs) were living in the main house with their uncle. Also living with Zephaniah in 1830 was his nephew Charles J. McNeill, the son of his sister Martha and her husband, Daniel McNeill. Martha Kingsley McNeill was also a frequent guest at Fort George Island.

In addition to serving as the residence for Anna and her children, the "Ma'am Anna House" was the food-preparation center for the main residence. The southeast room on the ground floor had an oversize fireplace and hearth that was designed for food preparation on a scale beyond the needs of just Anna and her children. Gertrude Rollins Wilson, whose father, John Rollins, purchased Fort George Island in 1868, speculated in the 1950s that food for residents of the main house was prepared in its basement kitchen and carried upstairs to the dining room. This is doubtful, however, given the basement's cramped quarters, its limited air circulation and natural lighting, and the heat and bustle such activity would have generated. It is more likely the food was prepared in the "Ma'am Anna House" and carried next door to a basement warming kitchen. That would be consistent with Wilson's description of a tabby walkway (tabby is a concrete-like material) between the Anna and Zephaniah houses, "bordered by oleanders, crepe myrtle and orange trees."[9]

Wilson remembered that the 1880s appearance of "Ma-am Anna's House was about as at present [early 1950s] except that the roof of the piazza did not connect with the main roof but stopped under the second story windows, the stairs having the usual roof over them protruding from the piazza roof." Wilson was born on the island in 1872, lived there during her childhood and early adult years, and continued

12. The "Ma'am Anna House" at Kingsley Plantation. Built of tabby bricks on the first floor and wood frame above, the dwelling had a kitchen and parlor on the first floor and bedrooms on the second. Photo by Judy Davis.

to visit until her death in 1956. Stories that she must have heard from former slaves who lived at Fort George Island when she was a girl led her to believe that the north room on the first floor "was at that time divided into two rooms, probably used as parlor and sitting room." The second floor had bedrooms on alternate sides of the stairway landing, on the north for Anna and on the south for the children.

Gertrude also remembered significant ornamental landscaping that was most probably in place when Anna Kingsley occupied the house. To the north and west stood a "fine grove of old and prolific lemon trees, [while] west of Ma-am Anna's House were orange trees and the remains of a flower garden screened from the cemetery by a thick hedge of bitter-sweet orange trees. In the cemetery grew narcissus, jonquils, old rose bushes and a very tall date palm tree."

Anna would have seen the cemetery when she looked behind (to the west of) her house. It is not known which owner of the island established the cemetery, nor whose remains were interred there, but the sight of the headstones apparently offended the aesthetic sensibil-

13. The "Ma'am Anna House" also functioned as a "kitchen house." Food was prepared in the ground-floor kitchen and carried to the main house on the right. Photo courtesy of the National Park Service, Timucuan Ecological and Historic Preserve, Jacksonville, Florida.

ity of Wilson's mother. They were removed and placed horizontally under a thick layer of dirt.

Located directly south of the "Ma'am Anna House" were a large well and a "grove of purple and white fig trees." To the east and "in front of Ma-am Anna's House was a large group of bananas, several large orange trees and crepe myrtle trees. In the yard between the two houses [were] the remains of a somewhat formal planting, a century plant, lantanas, &c."

A white picket fence surrounded both dwelling houses. Outside the fence, "the avenue of cedars running east was in its prime, [and] laurel oaks formed an avenue to the stables and also towards the [slave] quarters." In the space between Anna's house and the slave quarters stood two large shade trees, both live oaks.

Anna and her children lived within the owner's portion of the building complex, in a separate dwelling located sixty feet southwest of Zephaniah's house. Constructed of tabby bricks on the first floor and wood frame above, the "Ma'am Anna House," as it came to be called, provided the spatial separation that Anna would have expected based on her experiences with polygamous families in Africa. Wolof wives and their children traditionally lived in separate houses located beside the dwelling inhabited by the husband. On the evenings when one of the wives slept in the dwelling of her husband, her children were cared for by another of his co-wives.[10]

In these comfortable and attractive surroundings, Anna watched her children grow up on the island. George, nearly seven years old when the family arrived, had playmates in the slave quarters, horses to ride, fishing expeditions in the surf and rivers, and the heavily forested sections of the island to hunt for small game. George lived for more than two decades at Fort George Island, learning from his father and the drivers how a plantation should be managed. He became the owner of Fort George Island in 1831. That same year he married Anatoile Françoise Vantrauvers and began rearing his own family.[11]

Martha and Mary could hike to Mount Cornelia, the highest point on the island, where they could play amid brightly colored butterflies and wildflowers. From the hill, ships could be seen as they approached the mouth of the St. Johns River, and at low tide miles of white, sandy beaches and numerous aquatic birds were visible. Many different species of birds frequented the island, changing with the seasons.[12]

Huge oyster-shell mounds stood prominently at the southern tip of the island. These were refuse heaps left by the Native American peoples who preceded the Timucua Indians, who occupied northeast Florida when the first European explorers arrived in Florida. The refuse heaps were in place centuries before the Timucua nation was formed. After Spain colonized East Florida in the sixteenth century, Fort George Island became a Catholic mission settlement.[13]

John Bartram visited the island in 1765, when East Florida was a British colony. Accompanied by his son William, who later became a naturalist of enduring fame, John Bartram toured the ruins of the village established by Franciscan missionaries for the Timucua Indians. Bartram wrote in his travel journal that the street configurations and building foundations were still in place at the mission site.[14]

Between 1763 and 1784 Fort George was a successful indigo plantation. The Kingsley children, arriving only three decades later, must have found wild patches of indigo at remote locations on the island where seeds had been scattered by birds. They certainly would have explored the ruins of the Spanish mission village located only one mile south of the slave quarters. A sand road led south from the stables and slave houses through the mission site and on to the shell mounds at the southern tip of the island. Piled forty feet high, the mounds covered an area as large as a modern football field.

The road connected at its south end to a causeway leading to Pilot Town on Batten Island, also known as Little Fort George Island, where ships stopped to leave mail and occasional visitors, and to load plantation produce. Each day channel pilots rowed out from Pilot Town to meet incoming ships and guide them safely around the sandbars that sometimes impeded entry to the St. Johns River. The arrival of ships and visitors, the unloading of cargoes, and the activities of the channel pilots would have made Batten Island an exciting place for children to visit.[15]

The sound of palm fronds as the wind stirred the trees lining the roadway south of the slave quarters held special memories for Anna's daughter Mary. In the 1880s, long after she had married John S. Sammis and moved away from Fort George Island, Mary still recalled helping her mother plant long rows of palms on each side of the road leading to the dwellings. The actual labor of digging and planting was no doubt accomplished by slaves, but what Mary Sammis clearly remembered was the beauty of the trees as well as the sound of the long palm fronds blowing in the wind, alerting her that she was nearing home.[16]

Under the management of Anna and Zephaniah Kingsley, the plantation buildings at Fort George Island were greatly expanded. Temporary shelters for the laborers were replaced by thirty-two permanent cabins built of a concrete-like material called tabby. Workers would shovel oyster shell into a combination of water, sand, and lime, and stir the mixture until it thickened. The substance was then poured into vertical wooden wall molds and left to harden. The molds were then removed, and the door and window frames were added, along with brick-lined fireplaces. Cedar-shake roofs were fashioned from trees cut on Fort George Island. Each cabin was divided into two rooms on the first-floor, with sleeping lofts above the eight-foot walls intended for family units.

14. A stereoscopic view titled "Palmetto Avenue, Fort George Island, Fla."
Mary Kingsley Sammis remembered helping her mother, Anna Kingsley,
plant the palm trees. Offshoots of these trees still line the road. Courtesy of
Kevin Hooper.

The availability of huge shell middens on the island made tabby
construction convenient and affordable. In addition to the slave cabins, the first floor of Anna's house and the stable were constructed of
either poured tabby or tabby bricks. Zephaniah Kingsley was familiar
with the use of tabby for building purposes from his time in South
Carolina, where the technique was well known. It is possible, however, that Anna Kingsley was responsible for tabby construction at
Fort George. She was from Senegal, where anthropologist Janet
Gritzner believes the technique originated. Gritzner has concluded
that Portuguese and Spanish travelers in the Senegambia first observed tabby construction in the fifteenth and sixteenth centuries and
carried the method back to the Iberian Peninsula. Eventually, it also
reached the Americas.[17]

Visitors to Fort George Island are often puzzled by the unusual
half-circle arrangement of the tabby slave cabins. Architects, preser-
vationists, and historians generally conclude the configuration was
part of a grand plan devised by Zephaniah Kingsley. The possibility
that Anna established the plan has never been advanced, and yet the
overall conception matches Wolof spatial usage and social patterns.

The cabins were uniquely arranged, placed on a carefully designed half-circle facing north toward the main dwelling house. Twenty-eight of the cabins measured twenty-one feet by fourteen feet, and each was spaced just twelve feet from its neighbor. The remaining four cabins were six feet longer and six feet wider than the others, the extra area intended as a reward to the plantation managers known as "drivers" (also enslaved men owned by Kingsley). Each driver cabin was set at a distance of twenty feet from its nearest neighbor.

The semicircular arc of cabins was intersected at its center by a sand road that ran north toward the dwellings of the owners and south toward the agricultural fields. Two of the larger cabins were placed at the center of the arc, on either side of the sand road. From each of these driver cabins rows of fifteen additional cabins extended east and west, the last being an oversized driver cabin. The two rows were a mirror image of each other. The end cabins faced inward and directly across from one another at a distance of approximately 200 yards, providing the drivers and all who occupied the cabins with an unobstructed view of the entire slave quarters.

This half-circle layout was rarely seen in slave quarters in the American South. Historic preservationist Wayne W. Wood has speculated that the design was intended to promote "privacy and individuality" for the families living in each cabin, suggesting that "the semicircular configuration of the cabins seems designed to benefit the quality of living for [the Kingsley] slaves and the development of a residential community among them."[18]

Others have concluded that the design was intended to maximize Kingsley's control of his laborers while maintaining a comfortable distance from them. His own dwelling was located 350 yards to the north. In the intervening space were vegetable gardens and small groves of fruit trees. Fig trees were planted in front of each cabin, and wells to supply fresh water were dug between every two cabins.[19] The author of an 1878 publication speculated that a slave "grave yard" once occupied a portion of the space between the two compounds, "placed there by Captain Kingsley, as tradition states, in order to prevent the slaves, who were excessively superstitious from leaving their cabins at night to steal corn from the barn."[20]

Master and slave lived apart, the historian Daniel Stowell has written, yet not so distant as to deny Kingsley "the best opportunity to observe and control his slaves."[21] Control may have been a motivation for the overall design, but it seems an insignificant one. Kingsley's dwelling was sufficiently distant from the slave cabins to minimize any control he might have exercised by direct observation. Further, because of his varied business enterprises, Kingsley was so often absent from the plantation that he placed day-to-day control in the hands of Anna and the drivers and overseers. If control was the motivation for the semicircular arc of the cabins, it is the placement of the drivers' dwellings that is essential.

These interpretations all overlook the possibility that Anna Kingsley may have influenced the design and placement of the tabby cabins based on African conceptions of human community and aesthetics. The Wolof villages of her youth featured family compounds with multiple dwellings, granaries, and other structures, all with entries facing an open area in the center. Each family compound was surrounded by a circular wall. The adjoining family compounds were similarly configured, and the entire village was surrounded by a circular wall. Historical archaeologist Brahim Diop, of Cheikh Anta Diop University in Dakar, Senegal, has concluded that the ravages of the slave trade forced the Wolof to reshape their villages for more effective defense against raiders on horseback, but until late in the eighteenth century the predominant structural design was circular.[22]

The building complex at Fort George Island is reminiscent of the circular African communities Anna knew in Africa. The residences of the masters, with the main house on the north end and wings on the east and west, reached back toward the semicircular arc of cabins occupied by the servants. Zephaniah's dwelling at the north end looked south toward the half-circle of slave cabins. Anna's dwelling was south and west of Zephaniah's and separated by a distance of sixty feet. Across from Anna's dwelling, to the south and east, a two-story barn and stable was constructed of tabby brick and poured tabby. Only the southern half was symmetrical in form, but the overall effect of the placement of the buildings resembled the circular shape of African communities familiar to Anna.

For a native of Jolof, the circular configuration may also have represented a form of security. Strangers who entered the compound from the south, on the road passing between the two drivers' dwellings, could reach Zephaniah Kingsley only after traveling through the entire slave village. The design also followed a pattern of deference to male authority seen among the Wolof, whereby the focal point of the village community was traditionally the dwelling of the master situated at the north end. According to Wolof paternal protocol, visitors would pass first through the men and women of the slave community before advancing to the residence of the "father," or family head. In March 2001 a delegation from the Ministry of Education of Senegal toured the ruins of the slave quarters at Kingsley Plantation. The leader of the group, Sidi Camara, said the design layout reminded him of rural Wolof villages, where the time-honored patterns of paternal protocol persist to the present.[23]

It is clear that Anna Kingsley's authority and influence at Fort George Island was considerable. Nevertheless, her domestic relationship with Zephaniah must have been complicated. She and her co-wives and their children lived in separate households and were part of the Kingsley extended family. During the 1830s Kingsley maintained simultaneous conjugal relationships with three, possibly four, women, Anna Kingsley, Munsilna McGundo, Sarah Murphy, and Flora Hannahan. Anna, Munsilna, and Sarah all lived with their children at Fort George Island, presumably in separate dwellings, while Flora and her children were given a plantation and residence at Goodbys Creek south of Jacksonville. Three white nephews of Zephaniah lived at Fort George Island on a semi-regular basis: Kingsley B. Gibbs and his brother Zephaniah C. Gibbs, and their cousin Charles J. McNeill. The boys learned plantation management at the island and retained close personal and business ties to Zephaniah until his death. When the nephews were in residence, and especially when accompanied by their parents, the main plantation house would have been crowded with white relatives. How these visits influenced the relationship between Anna and Zephaniah is a compelling question. Perhaps they added to Anna's determination to live in a dwelling separate from her husband's.[24]

On November 22, 1824, ten years after Anna Kingsley arrived at Fort George Island, John Maxwell Kingsley was born. John Maxwell

15. The tabby walls of the slave cabins still stand at Kingsley Plantation. Tabby, a concrete-like mixture of oyster shell, lime, sand, and water, was poured into wood forms and left to dry and harden. Each cabin was built to house one family. Photo by Joan E. Moore, December 1999.

was Anna's fourth and final child. He lived for thirteen years at Fort George Island.[25]

The boy was baptized on the island shortly after his fifth birthday in a unique ceremony celebrated by an unusual extended family. His sister Mary was godmother, and his uncle Zephaniah C. Gibbs was godfather. Baptized alongside John Maxwell was his niece, Mary Martha Mattier, the daughter of Fatimah McGundo Kingsley. Fatimah was John Maxwell's half-sister, the daughter of Zephaniah and co-wife Munsilna McGundo, who lived in a separate dwelling on the island. Fatimah conceived Mary Martha by Luis Mattier, a white planter living near Fort George Island. The wealthy planter José María Ugarte stood as godfather for Mary Martha; the child's godmother was Martha Kingsley, Anna's daughter and John Maxwell's sister. Two sons of African slaves were also baptized at this time. Presiding over this mix of races, cultures, and continents was Father Edward Mayne, an Irish priest who traveled from St. Augustine to perform the ceremony.[26]

Sacramental and ceremonial occasions were not part of the normal routine for Anna at Fort George Island. Children had to be cared for, and the domestic servants required supervision. Anna directed the labors of her own twelve slaves who lived at Fort George Island, and was often in charge of the entire operation. Anna's life was undoubtedly busy, but Zephaniah's frequent absences and continuing cohabitation with other women may have resulted in lonely times for her.

That was certainly the opinion of Susan Philippa Fatio L'Engle, a wealthy and influential white woman of cultivated tastes who may first have met Anna in 1814 or 1815, when they were both refugees living in Fernandina. L'Engle was the daughter of Francis Philip Fatio, Jr., whose family, like Anna's, had been driven away from a St. Johns River plantation by the Patriot insurgency. Only a child at the time, she had escaped with her family to St. Mary's, Georgia. After the violence subsided in northeast Florida, the Fatio family lived alternately at Fernandina and at San Pablo Plantation, the latter a few miles south of Fort George Island, until their plantation home at New Switzerland was rebuilt. Many years later Susan married John L'Engle, a West Point graduate, army officer, and prominent planter and lumberman in northeast Florida.

Following her marriage, L'Engle began making weekly trips to Fort George Island for afternoon visits with a woman whom she called "the African princess," who was married to "a wealthy planter and slave trader."[27] The writer Madeleine L'Engle, great-granddaughter of Susan Philippa Fatio L'Engle, left an endearing account of those visits in her book *The Summer of the Great-Grandmother.* Mrs. L'Engle was rowed by her own slaves to the Kingsley plantation at the mouth of the St. Johns River, where she quite properly began each visit by lunching with Zephaniah. Following the meal, she and Anna "went off together to the princess's rooms, and talked, and drank cold tea together."[28] It was her opinion that Anna felt "ostracized by both whites and blacks" and "nearly died of homesickness."

The memory of these visits, passed down through the generations of L'Engle family members, emphasizes Anna's loneliness. Such feelings would have been understandable, given her complete separation from her homeland and family of origin, and the circumstances of her life at Fort George Island. Further, these visits apparently occurred at the time Zephaniah initiated a sexual and familial relationship with Flora Hannahan, one of his slave women. Flora was eman-

16. This rebuilt cabin, larger than the others, was assigned to the family of one of four "drivers," slaves who supervised the other slaves. It anchored the eastern arc of thirty-two cabins arranged in a half-circle. Photo courtesy of the National Park Service, Timucuan Ecological and Historic Preserve, Jacksonville, Florida.

cipated on March 20, 1828. On the emancipation notice, she is described as "a mulatto-colored woman of twenty years of age, a native of Florida . . . about five feet high."[29] Only three days before Flora's emancipation, Kingsley had freed her mother, Sophie Chidgigine, the wife of Abraham Hannahan, formerly Kingsley's slave and plantation manager. Kingsley described Sophie as "a woman of Jalof, thirty-six years of age, about five feet high, black complexion."[30] Subsequently, Kingsley and Flora became the parents of several children.

What is most important about the family legend of Susan Fatio L'Engle's visits with "the African princess" is that it preserves the record of a unique friendship between a white and a black woman in a time when cross-racial bonding between women seldom occurred. Madeleine L'Engle writes that her "Greatie [Susan L'Engle] and the princess were close friends in a day when such a friendship was unheard of, and Greatie simply laughed when she was criticized and sometimes slandered because of this relationship."[31]

Susan Fatio L'Engle was a child of privilege on the East Florida frontier. Her parents and grandparents were European immigrants who achieved wealth and influence through their slave plantations in East Florida. The historian Susan Parker has described Francis Philip Fatio, Susan's grandfather, as an aloof and haughty frontier baron who treated even Spanish governors with a condescending disdain.[32] Madeleine L'Engle writes that her "Greatie spoke French, Italian, Spanish, German; read Latin and Greek" and "had a vast store of folk and fairy tales from all lands which she told and retold her children, grandchildren, and great-grandchildren."[33] She grew up in a household surrounded by books, flowers, and fine furnishings, and had servants to cater to her every need. Susan Fatio L'Engle could hardly

17. Building material for the tabby structures at Kingsley Plantation came from massive shell mounds like this one on Fort George Island. Oyster shells discarded by Native Americans centuries ago were shaped into ceremonial mounds and used in burial and religious ceremonies. Photo courtesy of Florida State Archives, Tallahassee.

have been unaware that she lived in a slave society that was drawing an increasingly rigid line between whites and blacks, yet she maintained a close friendship with a free black woman from Africa who had once been a slave. Susan and Anna rose above the degrading prejudices of the time.

The L'Engle family legend of the lonely African princess at Fort George Island also reinforces the compelling image of Anna Kingsley that emerges from the surviving Spanish and American records. It would have taken more than her pity for a lonely black woman to prompt Susan L'Engle to endure repeated journeys on the St. Johns River in order to pay afternoon visits. Anna Kingsley must have been an engaging conversationalist with remarkable life stories to share with this distinguished white lady. Perhaps initially drawn to each other by their shared experiences as refugees, the two women may have found their relationship was deepened by the dignity and intelligence that each brought to their weekly meetings.

Anna Kingsley was thirty-one years old when John Maxwell was born in 1824; Zephaniah was nearly sixty. East Florida had been a Spanish colony when Anna and Zephaniah commenced planting at Fort George; it was a territory of the United States when John Maxwell was born. The change of flags brought the stability and security that Spain had been unable to provide, prompting Zephaniah to purchase additional plantations. He was optimistic about Florida's economic future, but alarmed by the new system of race relations the Americans brought with them.

In 1823 Kingsley was appointed by President James Monroe to serve on East Florida's legislative body, the Territorial Council, an experience that increased his concern. Kingsley had supported the relatively liberal race laws of Spain, which encouraged owners to manumit their slaves and incorporate them into a three-caste society of whites, free people of color, and slaves. But the Americans arriving in the new U.S. territory in record numbers viewed all black people, whether slaves or not, as members of an inferior race and unworthy of freedom. The new society was to be composed of only two castes: free whites and enslaved blacks. There would be no place for free blacks.

Kingsley urged the Territorial Council to pass laws encouraging emancipation. Make the free colored people your allies, he reasoned, and enlist their assistance in controlling the much larger numbers whose labor was coerced. Instead, the assembly limited the right of free blacks to assemble, carry firearms, serve on juries, and testify against whites in court proceedings. Free blacks living outside of Florida were denied the right of entry. Town councils taxed free blacks unfairly and empowered sheriffs to impress them for manual labor projects. They could be whipped for misdemeanors, subjected to curfews, and even forced back into slavery to satisfy debts or fines.

Two new laws affected the Kingsley family directly. The first prohibited interracial marriages and made the children of mixed-race couples ineligible to inherit their parents' estates. The second imposed severe penalties on white men found to be involved in sexual liaisons with black women. In 1829 the assembly moved to curtail manumissions by requiring owners to forfeit $200 for each person emancipated, as well as to post a security bond for each. Within thirty days the freed person was required to emigrate permanently from Florida or risk being seized by the sheriff and sold back into slavery. Had this law been in effect when Kingsley freed Anna in 1811, he would have been forced to send her and the children away. Kingsley believed "the intermediate grades of color are not only healthy, but when condition is favorable, they are improved in shape, strength and beauty, and susceptible of every amelioration."[34] His children were intelligent and well-educated, yet the new laws categorized them as uncivilized and strictly regulated their activities. The motive seemed to be fear that free blacks might inspire slave rebellions.

The Kingsley family had some immunity since the residents of Spanish Florida at the time of cession received special legal protections under the Adams-Onís Treaty, but they could never be sure how the territorial courts would interpret the new laws. More importantly, Anna and Zephaniah's youngest son, John Maxwell, was born after Florida was ceded to the United States and had no special treaty protections. Wealth and influence might shield the family for a few years, but the future was ominous. Kingsley added a codicil to his will warning his loved ones of the "illiberal and inequitable laws of this territory [which] will not afford to them and to their children that protection and justice [due] in every civilized society to every human being." Keep a legally executed will at hand, he urged, until they could emigrate "to some land of liberty and equal rights, where the conditions of society are governed by some law less absurd than that of color."[35]

Alarmed by the rising tide of racism in Florida, Kingsley acted to protect the economic security of his family. Fort George Island was deeded to George Kingsley and his wife Anatoile in 1831. A clause in the deed decreed that Anna "shall possess the use of her house and whatever ground she may desire to plant during her life." A similar provision was inserted for Munsilna McGundo, who "with her daughter Fatimah, shall possess the use of her house and four acres of land—also rations during life."[36] In 1832 Anna was given the title to a 1,000-acre estate in St. Johns County at Deep Creek on the St. Johns River in exchange for "wages and faithful services during twenty five years together."[37] She still owned a 125-acre tract located in today's Mandarin south of Jacksonville on the St. Johns River and a 225-acre plot at Dunn's Creek granted by the Spanish government to compensate for her losses in 1813.

Flora Hannahan Kingsley was also provided a measure of financial security via property ownership. Kingsley deeded to her a 300-acre corn, cotton, and citrus farm on the south shore of Goodby's Creek, bounding his San Jose Plantation. Eventually, Kingsley would father six children by Flora.[38]

The Ashley and San Jose Plantations, valuable adjoining estates located on the east shore of the St. Johns River and immediately north of Goodby's Creek, became the property of Anna's daughters, Martha and Mary, although the titles were placed in their white husbands' names. Kingsley retained title to several other estates, including Reddy's Point, White Oak, St. Johns Bluff, Beauclerc Bluff, Drayton Island, and Laurel Grove. Until the end of his life Kingsley continued to act as patriarch of his extended family, selling properties and transferring titles as he thought best for the common interest.

Having distributed his properties to members of his family, Kingsley began investigating additional ways to protect them from Florida's racist climate. The fear that spread throughout the South after Nat Turner's 1831 slave rebellion in Virginia served as a warning to Kingsley that his family could be in danger if they remained in Florida. The

Second Seminole War of 1835–42 added to his worries by arousing racial hysteria and xenophobia among Florida's white residents. Blacks fighting alongside Indian warriors provoked special terrors among Florida slaveholders. Implacable foes in combat, the blacks among the Seminoles, many of them escapees from slave plantations in Florida and Georgia, joined in attacks on plantations before fleeing to remote forest and wetland retreats. St. Augustine residents were terrified in 1836 when they learned that some slaves residing in town had conspired with free blacks and Seminole Indians in a Seminole raid on a nearby plantation. Jacksonville's militia leaders, fearing "internal enemies" among their own black population, gave orders to keep under armed detention all slaves and free blacks not under the direct supervision of owners or guardians. The *Jacksonville Courier* warned that the "tragic scenes of Hayti" could be repeated in Jacksonville and that abolitionists were plotting to "deluge our country with blood." Free African Americans faced rigid restrictions, including severe punishments for anyone attempting to "teach any colored person to read or write."[39] Zephaniah Kingsley's resolve to move his family out of harm's way was greatly intensified by the events of the Second Seminole War.

Kingsley began traveling to northern cities to attend colonization and abolition meetings. When he rejoined his family, he brought news of a program initiated by the president of Haiti, Jean-Pierre Boyer, to recruit free blacks from North America to restore the prosperity Haiti had known before the slave rebellion of 1789–1803. Kingsley had become aware of the rich agricultural lands in Haiti during a three-year residency there in the 1790s. As the only free black republic in the Western Hemisphere, Haiti beckoned as a sanctuary from Florida's racial turmoil.[40]

Soon after his return from the North, Kingsley began transferring property titles again. It was decided that George would be the first of the Kingsley clan to move to Haiti, which necessitated the sale of Fort George Island to Zephaniah's nephew, Kingsley B. Gibbs. Eighty of Zephaniah's slaves were moved to the Ashley and San José Plantations, approximately five miles upriver from Jacksonville, and put to work under the supervision of another nephew, Charles J. McNeill. Most of the Kingsley family, including Anna, George and Anatoile,

John Maxwell, and Zephaniah's other co-wives and children, made plans to emigrate to the "Island of Liberty."[41]

Leaving Fort George Island was traumatic for Anna. She had lived there for nearly a quarter-century, longer than at any other location. Her fourth and final child, John Maxwell, had been born there and romped across the island for thirteen years. George had grown up at Kingsley Plantation, married at nearby St. Johns Bluff, purchased Fort George Island, and lived with his wife, Anatoile, in the house adjacent to his mother's dwelling. Martha and Mary progressed from adolescents to mature women during these years. They both married migrants from the northern states, white Americans of Scots ancestry, both stable and prosperous citizens. Martha married Oran Baxter, a shipbuilder and planter. Mary became the wife of John S. Sammis, a planter, sawmill owner, and merchant. Martha and Mary would remain in Florida with their husbands when Anna, George, and John Maxwell moved to Haiti.[42]

It was an emotional farewell for Anna. Isolated and secure, Fort George Island had been a place of refuge from the dangers of the Patriot era. But now the outside world intruded again, threatening the freedom of her family.

6 · Refuge in Haiti and Return to Florida

IN EARLY SEPTEMBER 1835 Zephaniah Kingsley traveled to Puerto Plata on Haiti's north shore. Situated on the eastern portion of the island, Puerto Plata had been part of the Spanish colony of Santo Domingo before the rebellion that drove away both France and Spain and established the first free black nation in the Western Hemisphere. Kingsley knew that the Republic of Haiti advertised itself as an "island of freedom" and a sanctuary from racism for free black men and women from other nations in the Americas.

Over the next three months the seventy-year-old Kingsley rode on horseback between Puerto Plata and the capital of Haiti, Port-au-Prince, a distance of more than 300 miles. En route he examined the quality of soil and timber and observed the ruins of scores of abandoned sugar plantations. The Haitian revolution that had ended three decades earlier left people of African descent in control of the island but unable to restore its former prosperity. Years of turmoil had destroyed a thriving export economy, and few citizens remained who were experienced with plantation management and commercial agriculture. Kingsley found "many superb and costly old plantations, with all their improvements and imperishable buildings of brick and stone, together with their valuable mill streams and water privileges convenient to towns, [that could] be purchased for a small part of what the improvements alone would cost."[1] He concluded that nothing could stop "the immediate development of the natural power and wealth of Haiti but its want of capital."

During a personal interview at the national palace with President Jean-Pierre Boyer, Kingsley learned that the government encouraged immigration of free persons of color from the United States and permitted them to lease land upon arrival. After a one-year residence, leaseholders would become eligible for Haitian citizenship and for legal purchase of Haiti's abandoned lands. Kingsley immediately arranged a leasehold for a 35,000-acre tract of land known as Mayorasgo de Koka, located at the eastern end of the island between Puerto Plata and the Yasica River. Kingsley would arrange a formal purchase of that estate in 1838 and place the title in the name of his eldest son, George.[2]

Kingsley had at last found a sanctuary for his family: Haiti would be the safe harbor where Anna Jai, his other wives, and his children could live untroubled by prejudice and discrimination. He returned to Florida in late November to begin planning a unique experiment in colonization. When tools, seeds, and other necessaries were assembled, Zephaniah sailed back to Haiti. On this voyage he was accompanied by his son George, whom he described as "a healthy colored man of uncorrupted morals, about thirty years of age, tolerably well educated, of very industrious habits," and by "six prime African men, my own slaves, liberated for the express purpose" of initiating the colony.[3]

The prospective colonists arrived at Cabaret Harbor in October 1836 and immediately began clearing land for cultivation. In the next few months the men planted corn and "sweet potatoes, yams, cassava, rice, beans, peas, plantains, oranges, and all sorts of fruit trees." The wives and children of George Kingsley and the indentured laborers arrived in October 1837.[4]

Anna Kingsley and her youngest child, John Maxwell, arrived at Cabaret Harbor sometime in 1838 and immediately moved into "commodious dwelling houses" in George's family compound.[5] By 1842 nearly sixty persons had migrated from Zephaniah's estates in Florida, including at least two of Zephaniah's other wives and their minor children. Flora Hannahan Kingsley and Sarah Murphy Kingsley left the racial strife in Florida to occupy houses in Puerto Plata and tracts Zephaniah set apart for them on the east and west boundaries of Mayorasgo de Koka.[6]

According to Zephaniah, Mayorasgo de Koka was from the outset a harmonious and prosperous estate, with the laborers sharing in the profits and acquiring lands of their own. Inland from the beach and harbor, a coastal plain of rich soils supported sugar and cotton production, citrus groves, corn and vegetable gardens, and cattle grazing. Flowing from its source in the heavily timbered mountains that enclosed the coastal plain, the Yasica River wound through the tract on its way to the ocean. Connecting streams reached into rich mahogany and cedar forests and provided the setting for a sawmill. Mahogany sawed there was transported to Puerto Plata for shipment to Europe and the United States. One of these, Cabaret Creek, fed the deep freshwater lake where George Kingsley located his settlement; then it meandered through orange groves, gardens, a royal palm and plantain walk, and meadows and cane fields before merging with the Yasica River. In July 1842 Zephaniah described Mayorasgo de Koka as set "in a fine, rich valley, heavily timbered with mahogany all around, well watered, flowers so beautiful, fruits in abundance, so delicious that you could not refrain from stopping to eat, till you could eat no more. My son has laid out good roads, and built bridges and mills; the people are improving, and everything is prosperous."[7]

In addition to a dwelling in the settlement on Cabaret Creek, Anna had a beach cottage at Cabaret Village that descendants in the Dominican Republic recalled in interviews in 1994 and 1995 as a place where Anna would relax wearing long cotton gowns and gold jewelry in styles she remembered from her days in Jolof. Anna lived in comfort at Cabaret from shares of the proceeds of Mayorasgo de Koka, supplemented with her own income from rentals of her slaves and lands in Florida. These were times of comfort and prosperity for Anna Kingsley, but like the other brief periods of peace and tranquility she had known in her life, they were destined to end too soon.

In 1843 Zephaniah, then in his late seventies and sensing his life was nearing its end, made arrangements to apportion the land and wealth he had acquired in Haiti. He divided the lands among his children and

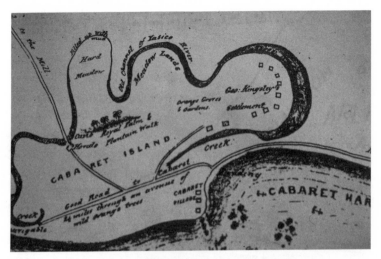

Map 3. Residential compound at Mayorasgo de Koka, Haiti, headquarters for a 36,000-acre estate acquired by Zephaniah Kingsley for his black wives and mixed-race children. Anna Kingsley resided at the George Kingsley Settlement and at Cabaret Harbor. Map drawn by Zephaniah Kingsley. Courtesy of the P. K. Yonge Library of Florida History, University of Florida, Gainesville.

asked his eldest son, George, to assume the responsibility of being guardian of all the minor children of Anna M. Jai, Flora Hannahan, and Sarah Murphy Kingsley. His wives were promised generous shares of the profits from the estates, but to protect them from racial prejudice in the United States they were told that if they moved away from the "Island of Liberty" they would forfeit all rights to share in the proceeds of Kingsley's properties in Haiti.[8]

When Zephaniah Kingsley sailed from Haiti in 1843, he said goodbye to his wives and children for the last time. On September 13, 1843, at age seventy-eight, the man who had been a maritime merchant, planter, slave trader, abolitionist, founder of a colony for freed slaves, and advocate of miscegenation and polygamy, died in New York City from pulmonary disease. Anna was fifty years old at the time and living a prosperous and tranquil life in Haiti.[9]

In 1846, three years after the death of her husband, Anna Kingsley decided to forfeit her life of comfort at Cabaret in Haiti and return to Florida. In addition to properties in Haiti bequeathed to his children who resided there, Zephaniah Kingsley had also left a fortune in Florida for his wives and mixed-race children. In 1842, one year before he died, Kingsley had been sufficiently concerned about the security of his Florida property to tell an interviewer that, in the event of his death, he considered it "likely enough . . . my heirs would break my will."[10] On October 19, 1844, the will was contested, not by his heirs but by his sister, Martha McNeill. Consequently, in 1846, eight years after escaping the hostile racial climate of East Florida, Anna returned to confront an intimidating array of white attorneys and judges as well as a hostile sister-in-law who labeled Zephaniah's last will and testament "defective and invalid" and sought to have his "coloured legatees" barred from inheriting his estate.[11]

Kingsley's will stipulated that all of his assets remaining after his debts and incidental bequests were honored were to be divided into twelve equal shares. Seven shares were assigned to Anna M. Jai's family: one to Anna, four to George, and two to John Maxwell.[12] Flora Hannahan and her children would divide two shares, and Micanopy, the son of Sarah Murphy, would receive one share. The final two shares were assigned to two of Zephaniah's nephews, Kingsley B. Gibbs and Charles J. McNeill. In today's monetary values, Kingsley left an inheritance worth millions, enough to arouse the baser instincts of relatives not named as legatees.

Martha Kingsley McNeill, Zephaniah's youngest sibling and the widow of Dr. Daniel McNeill of Wilmington, North Carolina, appears to have contested the will on her own initiative. One of McNeill's sons, two daughters, and two nieces were listed as co-petitioners, yet none resided in Florida. One lived in St. Petersburg, Russia, and another in New Orleans. A niece, Sophia Gibbs Couper, twice asked the judge to remove her name from the lawsuit, writing, "I never wished or intended to have anything to do with the litigation of the will."[13] The nephews most intimately associated with Kingsley during his lifetime, Charles J. McNeill, Zephaniah C. Gibbs, and Kingsley B. Gibbs, were not parties to the challenge.[14]

Among other charges, Martha McNeill argued that key witnesses and attorneys were not present when the will was signed in Jacksonville on July 20, 1843. Kingsley had selected his son George and John S. Drysdale as executors; yet Judge John L. Doggett appointed Benjamin A. Putnam and Kingsley B. Gibbs instead, further evidence to McNeill that the will should be declared "defective and invalid and ought to be revoked and annulled." Her attorney, Thomas Douglass, asked that the executors be "strictly prohibited from paying out" any of the assets of the estate.

At the center of the court challenge was McNeill's argument that Anna Kingsley was "a negress" and that George Kingsley, John Maxwell Kingsley, Flora Kingsley, Sarah Murphy, and Micanopy Kingsley were "mulattoes and each a slave of Zephaniah Kingsley" until they "voluntarily and of their own free will and accord without any coercion whatever" migrated to Haiti. They had gained freedom as a result of the move to Haiti, but they could not legally return to Florida, where laws stipulated that "all free negroes and mulattoes are expressly prohibited from migrating to or becoming domiciled." Even if they had remained in Duval County, however, they were legally classified as "coloured" and were therefore barred from inheriting or controlling property. Martha McNeill contended that her brother's will should be ruled "null and void."

Anna did not return immediately to Florida to respond to the legal challenge. At first she left legal matters to her son George and her son-in-law John S. Sammis. Anna and George were content to correspond with Sammis and delegate responsibility to him. Still worried about racial discrimination, George consulted with a New York attorney on the feasibility of reestablishing residency in Florida.

In January 1846 George Kingsley traveled to New York to meet with John LaMotte, a merchant with long-standing ties to Zephaniah Kingsley. The purpose of that meeting has not been documented, but it was a prelude to momentous changes in Anna Kingsley's life. In February George boarded a merchant vessel headed for Puerto Plata. During the passage the ship was wrecked at sea, and George was drowned. Anna's husband and her eldest son died only twenty-nine months apart. It was this combination of family tragedies, coupled with the threat to the family's base of financial security in Florida, that prompted Anna to leave Haiti.[15] Her co-wives, Flora Hannahan and Sarah Murphy, remained in the Dominican Republic with their families, as did the widow and children of George Kingsley and her youngest child, John Maxwell Kingsley.

Returning to Florida was a risky venture, however. Anna had been corresponding with her daughters, Martha Baxter and Mary Sammis, and was aware that race relations had become increasingly tense as disputes between the slave and free states escalated. There was always the danger that customs officials at any port of entry she chose would refuse to admit her or detain her as a nonwhite alien.

The decision to return to Florida was perhaps made easier by new disturbances on the "Island of Liberty." A revolution drove Haiti's black rulers from the eastern portion of the island, and Spain resumed control of its former colony. A subsequent independence movement drove the Spanish forces away and led to the creation of the independent Dominican Republic. The north-shore region near Cabaret became the center of sporadic violence during these campaigns, and the citizenship rights of free persons of color were once again in question. Furthermore, the prosperity at Mayorasgo de Koka had begun to decline as timber resources were depleted and laborers drifted from the estate. Anna had been apprised of the dangers in the United States, and also knew that her right to share in the proceeds of Mayorasgo de Koka would be forfeited if she left the island. But Zephaniah's estate in Florida represented the greatest potential for her family and therefore justified the risk.[16]

On her return to Florida in 1846, Anna resided temporarily with one of her daughters while she searched for a residence of her own. Her old home, the "Ma'am Anna house" at Fort George Island, had been purchased by Kingsley B. Gibbs. Anna immediately became an active participant in the legal battles over Zephaniah's will and the management and distribution of his assets.

Deliberations in the case *Martha McNeill et al.* v. *Putnam and Gibbs* (as executors of Kingsley's estate) had begun in 1845 in the Duval County Circuit Court under Judge Farquhar Bethune. Unfortunately, documentation concerning Judge Bethune's ruling cannot be found due to a fire in Jacksonville in 1901 that destroyed most of the Duval County court records. The only secondary source that deals directly with the case is "The History of Zephaniah Kingsley and Family," written by James Johnson in the 1930s when he was a researcher for the Federal Writers' Project. Johnson concluded that Judge Bethune ruled in favor of McNeill's petition and that the Florida Supreme

Court upheld that ruling, in effect declaring Kingsley's will "null and void" and deciding against the interests of his black wives and mixed-race children. Johnson based his conclusion partly on a Florida Supreme Court case heard in 1883, *Kingsley* v. *Broward*, because the court record contained a copy of Kingsley's 1843 will. A closer examination of *Kingsley* v. *Broward*, however, reveals that the lawsuit was initiated by three sons of Zephaniah Kingsley and Flora Hannahan Kingsley (James, William, and Osceola), who were residing then in the Dominican Republic. The brothers brought a "suit of ejectment" against John and Adele Broward with the intention of recovering title to a farm that had once belonged to their mother. It is clear from the court record that this case had nothing to do with Martha McNeill's attempt to have her brother's will declared "null and void."

In fact, no Florida Supreme Court record exists concerning Martha McNeill's lawsuit. Apparently, circuit court judge Bethune ruled against the plaintiffs sometime in 1845, and lawyers for McNeill appealed that ruling to the Superior Court of the District of East Florida. In March 1845 hearings began in Judge Isaac H. Bronson's chambers at the courthouse in St. Augustine. In a legal motion filed before Judge Bronson in September 1846, Kingsley B. Gibbs, acting as an executor of Zephaniah Kingsley's estate, commented that McNeill's lawsuit had been "transferred" to the Superior Court sometime in 1845, and that "the court had pronounced a decree against the petitioners" in late March 1846. That judgment remanded the case back to the custody of the Duval County Circuit Court.[17]

In March 1846, therefore, Anna Kingsley received the heartening news from Judge Bethune that the Superior Court had ruled against Martha McNeill's petition. Zephaniah Kingsley's will had been affirmed and his sister Martha McNeill had been ordered to pay the court costs related to the trial. After the superior court's ruling, McNeill apparently terminated her challenges to the will. The result of Judge Bronson's ruling was to confirm the promise in the Adams-Onís Treaty of full citizenship rights to all free persons residing in the colony when Spain ceded East Florida to the United States. Zephaniah Kingsley's "colored" heirs and legatees were thus ruled eligible to inherit his estate.[18]

Once the inheritance and citizenship rights were guaranteed, Anna

Madgigine Jai Kingsley assumed control of the family's economic interests in the United States. She worked in consultation with John Sammis, her white guardian, as required by Florida statutes and the Jacksonville municipal codes. She chose an aggressive course of action concerning Zephaniah's estate. On August 21, 1846, Anna petitioned the Circuit Court for a distribution of assets to the legatees. The executors filed an accounting in September listing a cash balance of nearly $60,000 and considerable additional assets in the form of securities, outstanding loans, real estate, and human property. Judge William F. Crabtree ordered the real and personal property sold at auction on January 1, 1847, with the assets derived from the sale to be distributed to the heirs.[19]

Zephaniah Kingsley's estate continued to be probated in the Duval County courts for many years, its proceeds supplemented by loan and interest payments when claims for damages against the United States in the 1812 and 1813 "Patriot Rebellion" were paid by the U.S. Treasury. The legatees, including those remaining in Haiti, each received thousands of dollars in payments supervised by the court. Their signed receipts still remain on file.

Anna continued to petition the court and to manage the assets of Zephaniah's estate to the advantage of herself and the other legatees. She was successful in having her own slaves separated from the workforce at San Jose and returned to her personal supervision. Landed property similarly deeded to her was also returned to her control.

In a surprising action in 1847, she brought suit to remove Zephaniah's nephew, Charles J. McNeill, from his job as overseer of San Jose Plantation. McNeill had been reared at Kingsley Plantation and Anna had known him for most of his life. McNeill appears to have modeled his life after Zephaniah's: He became a plantation manager and slaveowner, and chose a mixed-race woman, Elizabeth Coffee, to be his wife. Joshua Coffee, a white man and Elizabeth's father, was living at San Jose Plantation and helping with plantation management when Anna petitioned the court accusing McNeill of mismanagement and asking that he be relieved of his duties. The records of the probate court, specifically payments to overseers other than McNeill, indicate that Anna successfully argued her case.[20]

Anna also petitioned to have the land and slaves at San Jose rented out, arguing that operating the plantation under an overseer was producing less revenue than could be gained from renting the land and slaves separately to other planters. After an extensive investigation, which included the testimony of several prominent local planters, Judge Crabtree ruled against Anna's motion. Crabtree concluded that overwork, harsh treatment, and damage to their health would inevitably result if the enslaved men and women were rented out. It appears that at least in this instance, profits mattered more to Anna than the health and well-being of slave families. She was tough-minded when pursuing personal and family financial interests.[21]

Most historians have considered free black slaveowners to have been benevolent individuals who were primarily engaged in purchasing their own family members as a form of protection. That has been the opinion of Ira Berlin and John Hope Franklin, and especially Carter G. Woodson, who argued that free persons of color "purchased slaves to make their lot easier by granting them freedom."[22] Indeed, benevolence, family protection, and unification inspired several Duval County free blacks to emancipate slaves; but Anna Kingsley's efforts to rent the slaves at San Jose Plantation were clearly motivated by her interest in maximizing profits, not in making the slave's "lot easier." She would act differently on other occasions in the 1850s, but in this instance Anna Kingsley fit the pattern of materialistic black slaveowners whom Larry Koger studied in South Carolina. Koger concluded that "many black masters were firmly committed to chattel slavery and saw no reasons for manumitting their slaves. To those colored masters, slaves were merely property to be purchased, sold or exchanged. Their economic self-interest overrode whatever moral concerns or guilt they may have harbored about slavery."[23]

In January 1847 Anna Kingsley purchased a 22-acre farm on the east bank of the St. Johns River, across from Jacksonville. The farm, known as Chesterfield, was located midway between the estates of her two daughters. Part of the Branchester Tract, Chesterfield is today a key parcel of the Jacksonville University campus in the Arlington section of Jacksonville.[24]

In June of that same year, Anna sold a 1,000-acre plantation located at the junction of Deep Creek and the St. Johns River. Zephaniah had deeded that estate to her in 1832, along with four slave families. She owned at least one additional property in 1847, a tract on the east side of Dunn's Creek given to her in 1816 by the Spanish government in gratitude for her heroic actions during the "Patriot" insurgency. That tract had apparently not been cultivated as late as 1851, the year that it reverted to the State of Florida for "default of taxes."[25]

Henceforth, Anna Kingsley's life would focus on her family and on the section of Duval County located along the St. Johns River that is today known as Arlington. Entirely rural then, Arlington became a free black community unlike any other in Florida.

7 · A Free Black Community in a Time of Race Hysteria

AFTER RETURNING from Haiti, Anna Kingsley became matriarch of the Kingsley clan in Florida, exerting influence on her family's social and economic endeavors. Her economic interests focused initially on her deceased husband's estate and her farm, Chesterfield, and the fifteen slaves who worked its fields. Ironically, that farm was at the center of a rural free African American community unlike any other in northeast Florida. Located east of the St. Johns River across from the town of Jacksonville, the community stretched from Little Pottsburgh Creek on the south to Reddy's Point on the north, a distance of approximately seven miles, and also extended several miles eastward. More than seventy free African Americans lived in this neighborhood, in fifteen households of white, black, and mixed-race adults and children. Only in the towns of St. Augustine and Pensacola, both colonial capitals under Spanish governance, could free black communities be found with numbers comparable to those in this rural Duval County enclave.[1]

What is most striking about that rural community is that it flourished during the 1840s and 1850s, when an increasingly virulent race hysteria prompted many free blacks to leave the state. While Florida's numbers of free blacks remained relatively static from 1830 to

1860, increasing from 844 to only 932, they dropped as a percentage of total population from 2.4 percent to 0.6 percent. During these same years the state's total population increased fourfold, from 34,730 to 140,424. These trends were found throughout the lower South, where 98 percent of all African Americans were enslaved in 1860.[2]

In some regions of Florida the free Negro population declined markedly from 1830 to 1860. In St. Johns County, free blacks numbered 172 in 1830, roughly 7 percent of the county's total population. By 1860, however, their numbers had fallen to 82 (only 3 percent of the total population). Many decided their freedoms were endangered and emigrated to Cuba, Haiti, and elsewhere. In Pensacola the departures were even more dramatic: more than 150 free blacks moved to Mexico during the 1850s. Describing the emigrants as a "respected property-owning class," the *Pensacola Gazette* commented on April 4, 1857, "It was a painful sight to see them parting from their friends and native country to seek homes in a foreign land."[3] For the free blacks still in St. Johns County in 1860, over 90 percent resided in St. Augustine (up from 73 percent in 1830). In Nassau County, 86 percent of all free blacks resided in the town of Fernandina.

In Duval County, however, the free black population increased substantially from 1830 to 1860. In 1830, 86 free blacks resided in the county; thirty years later the count stood at 180. In 1860 more than 70 resided in the rural area east of the St. Johns River, near the estates of Anna Kingsley and her daughters. Unlike the other counties with free Negro populations, the proportion of town dwellers in Duval decreased in the period 1830–60, from 73 to 48 percent.[4]

As these population data suggest, free blacks fared poorly after Florida became an American territory. Efforts to institutionalize a two-caste system of race relations began soon after the change of flags. Blaming free persons of color for creating discontent among slaves, legislators in 1827 and 1828 passed laws barring them from joining public gatherings and from giving seditious speeches. Free black vendors were forbidden to conduct commercial activities on Sundays. Rights to carry firearms were restricted in 1825 and 1828, and taken away entirely in 1833. Free blacks were barred from jury service and from testifying against whites in court proceedings. Florida law prohibited interracial marriages and made the children of mixed-race couples ineligible to inherit their parents' estates. White men found to be involved in sexual activity with African American women could be fined up to $1,000 and deprived of their civil rights. Discriminatory head taxes were levied on all free black males over fifteen years of age; supplemental taxes were assessed in subsequent years by both state and municipal governments. Free blacks were even barred from entering the Territory of Florida.[5]

The council also moved aggressively to outlaw manumission. In 1829 slave owners were required to forfeit $200 for each person emancipated, and to post a security bond equal to the value of the slave being freed. Within thirty days of emancipation, the newly freed person was required to migrate permanently from Florida or risk being seized by a sheriff and sold back into slavery. Blacks already in the free population could be sold back into slavery to satisfy debts and fines arising from misdemeanor convictions.

To tighten the controls on persons of African descent even further, the council in 1842 passed a law requiring that all free blacks place themselves under the legal protection of a white guardian. When the guardian law was strengthened in 1848 and 1856, hundreds of free blacks emigrated. Those who remained were confronted with a new set of municipal laws that further eroded their rights. In Jacksonville new laws were passed permitting free blacks to be impressed for manual labor projects, whipped for misdemeanor offenses, restricted to a 9:00 P.M. curfew unless they carried passes from guardians, and barred from congregating without a permit from the mayor. If they failed to pay a $5.00 annual fee to register with their guardians, they faced between ten and twenty-nine lashes with a cowhide whip. In 1852 the fee increased to $10.50 and the punishment to thirty-nine lashes.[6]

As early as 1823, free persons of color in St. Johns County tried to block passage of racially discriminatory laws. They petitioned the territorial council in 1823, wrote letters to newspaper editors, and sought justice in the courts. St. Augustine resident and landowner Robert Brown wrote to the editor of the *East Florida Herald* in 1824, referring to himself as a native of East Florida and a man of "common sense." Brown recounted conversations with his white neighbors concerning the $8.00 annual poll tax levied by the county on free blacks age fifteen and older (whites paid only $1.00, levied when they reached age twenty-one). His neighbors justified the tax by saying, "such is the case in Georgia, an old and well regulated state," and they alleged that whites were expected to provide more services to the government than free blacks. Brown disagreed, calling the poll taxes "unequal" and "consequently unconstitutional," and he suggested that Georgia's laws had been passed to "fence and shore up" the evil of slavery in that state: "Whites as well as colored men of this county ought to deprecate precedents from the negro laws of Georgia, as they would from the blue laws of Connecticut, that tried witches by dunking and flogged husbands for kissing their wives on Sunday."[7]

Brown conceded that free blacks had none of the burdens that came with "elections and legislations," but pointed out that they were also barred from any participation in self-government:

> If we have none of the burdens of jurors, neither are we tried by our peers. If we have none of the cares, labours, responsibilities and dangers of civil and military offices neither have we any of their profits and honors. But they say we have more time. This is true. But how is it so? Why they have taken all else to themselves and left us only time as the consideration. It is not that we would not take our part in all these and glad of the opportunity of doing so but we are declared so far degraded as to be rendered incapable. They would have us to pay for the degradation that has been laid on us? This would be the effect of any taxation or contribution bearing unequally on us.[8]

At least one white official agreed that the new poll taxes were discriminatory. In November 1824 County Court Judge Joseph L. Smith ruled on a petition from James Clarke, a free black from St. Augustine who was seeking to stop the county from collecting a "discriminatory and unconstitutional" poll tax. On November 24 the *East Florida Herald* reported, "Judge Smith has decided in favour of the petitioner."

Stymied at the county level, advocates of a poll tax on free blacks transferred their campaign to the territorial council. In 1828 the council passed a law authorizing counties to impose poll taxes on free blacks. James Clarke promptly challenged the constitutionality of the law, joined by four of his brothers, also free blacks, as co-plaintiffs, and his white father, George J. F. Clarke, as principal witness.[9]

These discriminatory laws impelled Zephaniah Kingsley to send his free black wives and children away from Florida to reside in what he thought was an "island of liberty," the free black Republic of Haiti. But prior to this move, Kingsley joined with other whites in futile attempts to deter the rash of invidious legislation. He served on the 1823 territorial council, but was unable to persuade other delegates to adopt the more flexible Spanish racial policies. Kingsley addressed the council as a concerned citizen in 1828, and wrote a persuasive essay on the benefits of continuing the three-caste system of the Spanish era. These efforts failed as well, and by 1829 a two-caste system of race relations was on the statute books in Florida.[10]

For a few years after that, it was still possible to persuade sympathetic court officials to ignore the anti-emancipation law and permit the more flexible practices of the previous Spanish government to continue extra-legally. By the late 1840s, however, after slave values had increased dramatically and politicians began advocating a revival of African slave importations, circumvention of anti-manumission laws had become unpopular. In the decade of the 1850s, which brought significant economic and demographic changes as well as sectional crises and secessionist agitation, free African Americans became the victims of rising race hysteria.

Cases were brought in the Duval County courts in which individuals challenged the wills of their deceased siblings and sought to enslave their own nephews and nieces. For example, eighty-four-year-old John Sutton hired a Jacksonville attorney in 1846 to draw up a will to free his slave wife and their fourteen children and grandchildren in compliance with Florida law. Sutton willed that his properties be converted to cash assets and given to his family, whom he wished to migrate to a northern state.[11]

After Sutton's death, however, the children rejected migration and opted instead to stay at their Black Creek home, confident that "nobody would trouble them."[12] But trouble soon arrived in the person of their paternal uncle, Shadrack Sutton, who traveled from Georgia to claim ownership of his brother's family. At the ensuing court inquiry, the elder sons of John Sutton told Judge William Crabtree they would heed their father's warning and migrate to a nonslave state to avoid becoming slaves of their uncle.

In 1851 Anna Kingsley's son-in-law, John Sammis, became caught up in a controversy involving the emancipated children of another white planter. Sammis and Isaiah D. Hart arranged a $4,000 security bond to release the free mixed-race children of Jacob Bryan from jail. Bryan, murdered in 1848, had manumitted his wife, Susan, and their children during his lifetime; but after his death, they were mistaken for slaves and incarcerated by the sheriff. Hart, the clerk of court who had issued the manumission papers, pointed out the mistake and the family was released. Soon thereafter, however, John Bryan and Mrs. Amaziah Archer, brother and sister to the deceased, arrived from Georgia to file a lawsuit contesting the free status of the mixed-race family. Archer and Bryan charged that the family had been freed in violation of the 1829 emancipation law. As Jacob's only white relatives, Archer and Bryan claimed they were the only "legitimate" heirs and were therefore legally entitled to inherit all of his property, including his slave wife and eight children.[13]

William Crabtree, judge of the Duval County Circuit Court, initially decided the Bryan case in favor of the defendants, but the ruling was appealed to the Superior Court of the Eastern District of Florida. Judge Thomas Douglass affirmed Judge Crabtree's ruling; but he also concluded that Susan, the eldest child of Jacob and Susan Bryan, came under a different interpretation of the Florida statute since she had been born in Georgia and brought into Florida as a slave. Judge Douglass issued orders to sell Susan back into slavery.[14]

Hoping to gain ownership of all in their brother's mixed-race family, Bryan and Archer appealed Judge Douglass's ruling to the Florida Supreme Court. In 1851 Judge Albert G. Semmes wrote for the court majority, "The conviction upon the public mind is settled and unalterable as to the evil necessarily attendant upon this class of population, and although treated by our laws humanely, they have always been regarded with a distrust bordering on apprehension—a class of people who are neither freemen nor slaves, their presence at all times deleterious and often dangerous to the public welfare."[15] The justices decreed that the emancipation papers Jacob Bryan obtained for his

family during his lifetime were invalid; once again an order was issued to sell his wife and children back into slavery.

By the time the sheriff of Duval County attempted to implement
Judge Semmes's ruling, Dennis and Mary Bryan had absconded. The
February 1852 sale of their sister Susan in front of the Duval County
courthouse, as a result of Judge Douglass's earlier ruling, undoubtedly encouraged them to leave the area. Unfazed, John Bryan and
Amaziah Archer sued the men who had posted bail for Dennis and
Mary, Sammis and Hart, hoping to recover the value of the missing
slave property. In 1853 the court awarded $900 as reimbursement for
the value of Dennis, whose whereabouts were then unknown. The
fate of Mary and the other family members is not discussed in the
documents.[16]

After these court decisions regarding the wife and children of
Jacob Bryan, Florida's law enforcement officials and lower court
judges showed less ambiguity when interpreting the 1829 manumission prohibitions. Historian Eugene Genovese observed that similar
rulings throughout the slave states served a hegemonic function, forc-
ing individual citizens to subordinate their consciences to the will of
state legislatures and judicial rulings. Genovese contends that individuals were forced to submit "to the collective judgment of society.
It [the law] may compel conformity by granting each individual his
right of private judgment, but it must deny him the right to take action based on that judgment when in conflict with the general will."[17]
The 1829 anti-manumission law that so troubled Zephaniah Kingsley
had become the general will two decades later. The Florida Supreme
Court had effectively barred the gate to freedom for enslaved men,
women, and children. In subsequent years manumissions would be
exceedingly rare.[18]

The historian Ira Berlin found that challenges to emancipations
were frequent throughout the South in the 1850s, a period when com-
mitment to slavery intensified as cotton cultivation spread across the
region. High profits and slave shortages drove up prices, and "bitter
relatives, fuming over lost inheritance, often went to court and de-
prived slaves of their promised freedom."[19] Florida's 1859 law encouraging free Negroes to choose masters and to re-enslave them-

selves voluntarily was in keeping with trends throughout the South.[20]

Such sentiments were emphatically expressed in a July 12, 1851, editorial in the St. Augustine *News*, which attacked free blacks as "useless" troublemakers and "hopeless, degraded, wretched, and forbidden outcasts." White hysteria erupted in Jacksonville in 1852, following a failed runaway attempt by three enslaved sawmill laborers. Angry citizens condemned "abolitionists and their tools," whom they suspected of "attempting to entice our slave population to abscond."[21] Alarmed white working men called for hefty license fees for the town's free black laborers, and for restrictions on "hired out" slaves who were living apart from their owners. Unless African Americans were "kept and restrained within their proper limits" (meaning slavery), the alarmists claimed, insurrections would threaten the lives of white citizens.[22]

Racist attitudes had hardened by 1855, when Edwin E. Alberti, a sawmiller owner and planter on the St. Marys River, found himself in the middle of a nasty public brouhaha. In 1849 Alberti had emancipated a teenage girl named Jessie (Alberti). Under Florida law Jessie should have migrated from the state within thirty days of gaining her freedom, but instead she stayed at the Alberti plantation to work for wages. Her work was so satisfactory that Alberti and his wife praised her "moral worth, purity of conduct, strict integrity, and unwavering veracity," and made "very sufficient provisions" for her in their wills.[23] Jessie said her goal in life was to become a missionary in Africa, but in 1855 a mysterious illness forced her to travel to New York City for medical treatment.

Alberti accompanied Jessie to New York City. He later reported that when they arrived at their hotel, he was surprised to find his former overseer waiting at the desk. The young white man immediately claimed Jessie as his lover and intended wife; and before the startled (so he reported) Alberti could intervene, the couple hurried away to be married. Alberti returned to Florida and mailed a wedding announcement to a Jacksonville newspaper referring to the bride as "Miss Jessie Acker." Reference to the bride's race was omitted from Alberti's letter and the published newspaper announcement.[24]

Public reaction to the announcement was severe. In a letter to the editor, one writer denounced "such dark proceedings that our negro girls be classed upon a footing with young ladies of the South, who are generally termed Miss or Misses."[25] Another writer ranted about Alberti's "outrage of disrespect to the South" and labeled the Nassau County mill owner an "abolitionist and total nuisance to the feelings of the South."[26] Alberti's apologies appeared in later issues of the newspaper, but they could not appease the angry defenders of Southern honor. On August 5, 1855, at a public meeting in Jacksonville, Alberti was denounced as "an enemy to the South" and advised to "rest beside his protegee."

During the 1850s white men and women in northeast Florida were fanatically intent on enforcing the racial taboos of their society. Judge Semmes's 1851 opinion for the Florida Supreme Court in the Bryan case constituted legal endorsement for their racist sentiments. Further institutional support came in 1853, via Florida Supreme Court Justice Leslie A. Thompson's ruling in the case of "Luke, a Slave, Plaintiff in Error, vs. The State of Florida." In Thompson's judgment it was important that "the superiority of the white race over the African negro should be ever demonstrated and preserved [and] the degraded caste should be continually reminded of their inferior position. . . . There is an obvious propriety in visiting their offenses with more degrading punishment."[27] It was clear to all observers that white supremacy had become the "general will" in Florida.

As these racist sentiments intensified, a free black community formed and thrived in a rural area of Duval County. At the core of that community was an aging African-born woman, Anna Madgigine Jai Kingsley, the matriarch of an extensive mixed-race kinship group. Anna's primary concern was the safety and well-being of her daughters and grandchildren. In 1848 she arranged the baptism of her grandchildren Emma Jane, Julia Catherine, and Osmond Edward Baxter at the Catholic Church in Jacksonville. Another grandchild migrated from the Dominican Republic sometime during the 1850s to live with Anna at Chesterfield. Isabella (also called Bella), the daughter of John Maxwell Kingsley, was eleven years old and still living with her grandmother when the 1860 Duval County census was taken.[28]

Anna Kingsley continued her deceased husband's practice of

emancipating enslaved men and women for meritorious service or for payment of half their appraised value. Lindo and Sophey Kingsley, along with their children Labo, George, and Philip, were liberated in the 1850s. Also emancipated were Abdallah and Bella Kingsley and their children Paul and Amie. Both families were free and living near Anna and her daughters when the 1860 Duval County census was recorded.[29] They were fortunate that sympathetic court officials issued freedom papers to them in defiance of the law. The newly freed families also remained in Duval County well beyond the thirty-day deadline stipulated in the anti-manumission provisions of the 1829 Florida statute. The Duval County sheriff did not arrest them and sell them back into slavery. Both families settled in close proximity to Anna Kingsley and her kinship network and participated in the life of the rural free black community.

How these emancipations were possible cannot be determined from the incomplete historical record that remains to us, but one obvious and vital factor was the cooperation of white persons with wealth and power who were willing to provide legal and social protection and economic patronage. Drawing on long-standing personal relationships with the ruling elites of northeast Florida, men like Zephaniah Kingsley had provided such protection prior to the 1840s. After Kingsley's death in 1843, John Sammis, his son-in-law, apparently provided similar support. Other white men were supportive, in particular Isaiah D. Hart and Francis Richard, but it was Sammis who acted as guardian and protector for Anna Kingsley, her daughters and grandchildren, and the other free blacks living in the vicinity.

One notable member of that community, known as Carpenter Bill, had once lived at San Jose Plantation as Zephaniah Kingsley's slave, where he had managed to win some degree of independence for himself. With a reputation as a skilled and dependable house builder, Carpenter Bill was frequently hired out to white planters of the region; but he would consent to do the work only if he personally approved his prospective employer, and only then if he was permitted to select a man to assist him and if the employer agreed to pay the two men in cash at the end of each workday. The assistant he chose was Bonify, the head of another family owned by Kingsley. Slave "hire-out" was not unusual in antebellum Duval County. Numerous examples of men, women, and children hired to work for wages for an employer other than their owner can be found in the probate files in the courthouse. What is unique about the experiences of Carpenter Bill, however, is that he made independent arrangements and held veto power over prospective employers and that the wages were paid directly to him, rather than to his owner or an executor.

Following Zephaniah's death, Carpenter Bill and his family were listed on a March 13, 1844, inventory of slave property in the Kingsley estate. Bill, his wife Hannah, and their children Frank, Alonzo, Bill, Lavinia, and Marianne were appraised by the Duval County sheriff as having a combined value of $3,605. Apparently, Bill had been saving the income generated by his carpentry work because shortly after the inventory was conducted he purchased freedom for himself, his wife, and their daughter Marianne.[30] George Kingsley, who inherited more than eighty slaves, continued his father's policy of permitting slaves the right of self-purchase for half of their appraised value. That only three family members were emancipated in 1844 undoubtedly reflects Bill's inability to save the $1,800 it would have required to free all of the others. But this resourceful African-born man continued to save his earnings and purchase freedom for his children.

On February 1, 1848, a second Kingsley estate auction was held, this time prompted by the death of George Kingsley. Four children of the former slave carpenter were listed in the inventory of slave property. William Kingsley was among those attending the auction held in front of the Duval County courthouse. He had evidently been able to save $400 during his four years of freedom, for when Alonzo was led to the auction block, his father was the high bidder. In one of many dramatic moments in Florida history, a free black man named William Kingsley purchased his own son at a slave auction. In the weeks that followed, and in violation of the 1829 law restricting emancipation, Alonzo was manumitted and allowed to remain in Florida. The old network of personal ties was evidently still functioning in contravention of state law.[31]

At this same estate sale William Kingsley could only watch and listen as the auctioneer sold a slave family composed of "Mike, Lavinia and infant Larry" for a high bid of $1,300. Lavinia was William's daughter. Mike was one of two adult sons of Jenoma and Jenny, a slave family also owned by Kingsley. They had been valued at $1,100 in the 1844 inventory of San Jose Plantation conducted after Zephaniah's death. Mike and his brother Augustus were appraised at $600 each. Between 1844 and 1848, Lavinia and Mike married and became the parents of a son.

Given the challenges facing a free black man in Florida in the 1840s, the wages William Kingsley could earn at his trade, and the high appraised value of his family ($3,605 in 1844, or more than $100,000 in today's currency), purchasing freedom for four members of the family was a significant achievement. Standing in front of the seat of justice for Duval County, Florida, on that winter day in 1848, William would have to watch as his daughter, son-in-law, and grandson walked from the auction block with a new owner, W. G. Christopher, who also purchased San Jose Plantation.[32]

Christopher may have permitted William Kingsley and his family to visit Lavinia; but if he feared that free blacks might incite his slaves to rebel, as some owners did, family visits could have been prohibited. As resourceful as William Kingsley appears to have been, it would have been difficult to keep his family unified without a sympathetic owner. Michael P. Johnson and James L. Roark argue persuasively that free blacks in the South walked a thin line between slavery and freedom, "always dependent on the sufferance of the white majority," always vulnerable if they failed to act with "decorum, piety, sobriety" or if they violated the "strict code of racial etiquette."[33] Acquiescing to the white majority position on slavery was at the core of that etiquette, and fraternization between free blacks and slaves could be seen as threatening, even when the slaves were one's children and grandchildren. Thus establishing and maintaining cordial personal relationships with powerful white men and women was vital.

In 1850 William, Hannah, and Mary Ann Kingsley composed one of the eight households of free persons of color living east of the St. Johns River and across from Jacksonville (today the area is called Arlington) who had formerly been slaves of Anna and Zephaniah Kingsley. Ten years later, William was living with his son Alonzo, who took the surname Phillips after being emancipated. Hannah, William's wife, was not enumerated. Her age was given as sixty in the 1850 census, and she may have died prior to 1860. Living close by in

1860 was a twenty-year-old mulatto woman named Mary Williams and her children Hannah and Nelly. Rebecca Williams, age thirty-five, also lived with them.

The 1860 census also lists a ninety-year-old African man, Toby Kingsley, as living alone in a house located in the same vicinity. Maria Kingsley, a forty-six-year-old black woman, lived nearby with her three daughters. Lindo and Sophia Kingsley and their children John and Iradina also lived in the neighborhood, as did Abdallah Kingsley and his wife, Bella, both African born.

When Anna Jai Kingsley is included in the count, at least six persons born in Africa were living in this free black community in the 1850s. It is unfortunate that so little is known about how their African heritages influenced their lives in America. Beyond sparse commentary about swimming outings by the slave boys at the Sammis plantation, and weekend dances attended by their parents, there is no information about the music, dance, art, culinary habits, or other cultural practices of the slave quarters or the free black households. The stories Anna Kingsley and her African neighbors told their African American children, grandchildren, and great-grandchildren have all been forgotten. The songs they carried in memory from Jolof and other parts of Africa to sing again in Florida are no longer remembered.

The sparse surviving documentation also makes it difficult to trace the relationships between Anna Kingsley's extended family and the surrounding free black community. It appears that the former slaves developed client-patron bonds with the Kingsley kin after they were emancipated. Anna and both of her daughters were estate owners in need of carpentry work, occasional day laborers, extra help at harvest time, and overseers. Both Anna and William Kingsley had been slaves together at Laurel Grove Plantation. She had seen examples of his handiwork at Laurel Grove and at Fort George Island. It would not have been surprising if, in the years after he was emancipated, Anna and her daughters sought him out when they needed carpentry work done. Like many social relationships Anna witnessed in the Americas, these, too, were reminiscent of Senegal, where patron-client ties often formed between Wolof slave owners and their liberated bondsmen. In both Senegal and Duval County, it can be assumed that traditional social distance and deference were maintained between slave owners and their former bondsmen, although frequent interaction undoubtedly occurred.

Equally intriguing is the nature of interaction between the freed persons in this community and the men and women who were still human property at the neighboring estates. Carpenter William Kingsley and his apprentice, Bonify Napoleon, are believed to have belonged to the Kamba ethnic group of southern Tanzania. Evidently they were enslaved together in 1806 and carried across the Atlantic in the hold of Kingsley's slave ship. The two men had known each other for more than forty years when William Kingsley was emancipated. It is hard to imagine ties of that duration ending when the freedom papers were issued. Bonify Napoleon and his family were purchased by John Sammis at the auction of George Kingsley's slave laborers on February 1, 1847, which meant that William and Hannah Kingsley, although free, lived in the vicinity of the slave quarters where Napoleon and his family were domiciled.

There is evidence of interaction between freed and enslaved blacks in the Arlington community, along with clues that family and social ties reached beyond the boundaries of individual plantations. In 1890, a quarter-century after the Civil War freed them from bondage, several men interviewed by a special examiner from the U.S. Pension Office recalled life on the Sammis Plantation. The examiner was in Jacksonville investigating a claim submitted by Albert C. Sammis, a lieutenant in the Colored Infantry during the Civil War who had suffered a rupture and was seeking a veteran's disability pension.

During the course of the investigation, it was revealed that Albert was the son of John S. Sammis and one of his slave women, Antoinette Paine. In 1844, after Mary Kingsley Sammis learned that Antoinette had conceived a child by her husband, she arranged to have Antoinette freed. When the child, Albert, was born on August 9, he was moved into Mary's household and raised with the other Sammis children. Antoinette was given property carved from the Sammis plantation, where she lived for more than forty years.

Albert recalled these circumstances during his interview with the special investigator. "This man Sammis was married to a mulatto

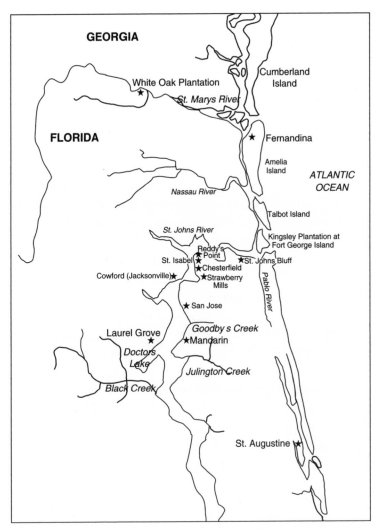

Map 4. Northeast Florida, showing the locations of estates owned in the 1850s by Kingsley family members and relatives: Anna Kingsley (Chesterfield), Mary and John Sammis (Strawberry Mills), Martha Baxter (St. Isabel), and Charles J. McNeill (Reddy's Point). These estates were at the center of a unique free black community.

woman and after Sammis got my mother in the family way she agreed to free my mother if Sammis would have no more children by my mother. This was agreed to before I was born but I was to remain with Sammis until I was twenty-one. He put me to blacksmithing and when the war broke out he went to New York and took me along."[34]

A dozen persons gave testimony, many of them former slaves or free blacks who had either lived at or visited Sammis Plantation before the war. Several had fond memories of swimming in the mill pond on Strawberry Creek. Alonzo Williams, a Jacksonville carpenter in 1890, said he taught Albert how to swim. Adam Robinson lived four miles away from the Sammis plantation, but went there regularly to visit, swim, and dance. Other men who gave depositions remembered regular Saturday night dances at the Sammis plantation attended by both slaves and free blacks. William Johnson lived four miles away and "came down Saturday nights and all day Sunday." He and Albert were close friends in childhood. The Sammis estate was apparently at the core of the black community north of Pottsburgh Creek, and its social activities attracted both slave and free.

Henry Adams had less fond memories of the plantation. He said he had known Albert Sammis "ever since he was born. Before the war I lived one mile from Colonel Sammis's place. I married one of Col. Sammis's slaves. Married several years before the war for I had three children sold away from me. I used to sleep on Sammis place most every night."[35]

Albert's half-brother, Egbert C. Sammis, said that he also swam with Albert and his friends. Egbert was a member of the Florida State Senate at the time the testimony was given. He acknowledged that Albert was his half-brother, but certainly not his equal in status. Senator Sammis remembered Albert as "one of the house boys."[36]

Egbert Sammis's aristocratic demeanor was in keeping with the circumstances of his childhood. His parents were among the wealthiest residents of Duval County. They owned a plantation of 8,000 acres along the St. Johns River and Pottsburgh Creek known as Strawberry Mills, which had once been part of a sawmill grant from the Spanish government. Sammis had worked for the sawmill owner, Francis Richard, prior to purchasing the property in the 1840s.

The Sammis estate abounded in live oak, cedar, and pine forests, and a sawmill, cotton gin, gristmill, and sugar mill (all powered by water) provided steady income. John Sammis boasted that many of Jacksonville's commercial buildings were constructed of bricks manufactured at his brickyard. The plantation also had 700 acres planted in Sea Island cotton, rice fields with dams and dikes in place, good summer and winter range for cattle and sheep, and an abundance of fish in rivers and creeks adjoining and intersecting the property.[37]

When Sammis attempted to sell the estate in 1861, he boasted of his large dwelling house and the many other houses and outbuildings on the property. There was also a large mineral spring and bathhouse, and a hydraulic ram that supplied water to the dwellings and extensive gardens.

The 1860 industrial census of Duval County estimated the annual output of Sammis's sawmill at 150,000 board feet of timber worth $10,000. In addition to his extensive land holdings, Sammis was one of Jacksonville's leading retail merchants, operating out of a store on Bay Street known as the Sammis Block. Each morning two slave boys rowed their master across the St. Johns River to his store on Bay Street, and each evening the same boys rowed him back to his home on the east shore.

Throughout the 1850s John Sammis received a tax bill based on the 8,000 acres he owned in Duval County. He was also taxed for thirty-six enslaved persons in 1840, sixty-six in 1850, and eighty-five in 1854. By the time the 1860 census was taken, Sammis had apparently sold his slave property and invested the proceeds in other ventures. Perhaps he feared the secessionist talk that was so common in Jacksonville by the late 1850s. His real estate holdings in 1860 were valued at $50,000 and his personal estate at $70,000, the latter reflecting the sale of his human property. He was investing in railroad and other stock and was a prominent supporter of the pro-Union political parties of the time: the Whig Party and its successors, the American Party and, in 1860, the Constitutional Union Party. John and Mary Sammis's children were educated by private tutors who lived at the family compound. As the children matured, they were sent to finishing schools and universities in the United States and Europe. It should not be surprising, therefore, that Senator Egbert Sammis would, in the 1880s, be somewhat patronizing toward his half-brother Albert.[38]

During the latter years of the 1840s and the decade of the 1850s, Anna Jai Kingsley lived at a farm located two miles north of the residence of her daughter, Mary Sammis. By 1860 she had sold that property and moved to Point St. Isabel, an estate two miles to the north owned by her eldest daughter, Martha Baxter. Anna was sixty-seven years old at the time, no longer a landowner, but still the owner of four slaves between the ages of nine and seventeen. Her assets were not insubstantial. In addition to the four slave children, she possessed $3,000 in cash and, as a result of a provision in Zephaniah Kingsley's will, the hope of additional riches through the one-twelfth part of Zephaniah's claim against the U.S. government for damages to Laurel Grove Plantation in 1813. (The principal had been paid, but claims for interest were still being considered.) She described herself as "feeble in strength" but "sound of mind and memory."[39]

Martha's husband, Oran B. Baxter, had passed away in 1847, leaving Martha in temporary financial difficulty. Baxter, a native of Cold Spring, New York, had lived in Duval County since at least 1830, when he was recorded by the census taker as a bachelor living with two other single men. By the time of the Second Seminole War (1835–42), Baxter was married to Martha Kingsley and operating a boarding house for soldiers at his father-in-law's St. Johns Bluff property. His own 347-acre St. Isabel Plantation, possibly a gift from his father-in-law, employed thirty-six slaves in 1840. Baxter purchased additional land, including part interest in a mill site, before becoming sick and unable to meet his obligations. Martha settled the debts after Oran's death, in part by contracting the labor of her slaves to her late husband's creditors.

In 1850 Martha was a forty-one-year-old widow living at St. Isabel Plantation with three of her children: Emma, age eleven; Osmond, eight; and Julia, six. Also living with Martha in 1850 was a white woman named Mary Ann Richard, the widow of wealthy planter Francis Richard, Jr., whose remaining lands were located at the junction of Little Pottsburg Creek and the St. Johns River, just south of Sammis. Mary Ann Richard's two children, Eugenia and Clinton, ages five and four, were also living at St. Isabel. Francis Richard, like Martha's father, had also had mixed-race wives and children whom he freed and remembered in his will along with his white offspring. The mixed-race Richard children were also part of the free black community located along the St. Johns River.

By 1854, seven years after her husband's death, Martha Baxter had paid off the debts of the estate and increased the number of slaves she owned from thirty-six to forty-eight. Four years later, her real estate was valued at $5,000 and her personal property, including slaves, at $27,500. Skillful at business and investments like her father had been, Martha Kingsley Baxter eventually became one of the ten wealthiest persons in Duval County.

Martha Baxter's St. Isabel estate had at its center a residential compound of multiple dwellings clustered in close proximity and occupied by her extended family and enslaved domestics. Sharing Martha's own domicile in 1860 were two of her daughters, Isabella Baxter and Anna B. Carroll. Anna's husband, Charles B. Carroll, was a white man from New York. Nearby, in a separate residence, was Martha's daughter Emma Baxter Mocs, her husband, Joseph Mocs, and two of their children. Mocs was a music teacher born in Hungary. Someone in the family performed on the viol, and no doubt other instruments were played at family gatherings. A second teacher lived in the Baxter compound in 1860, Miss Catherine Bullen, a white woman from South Carolina.[40]

Anna Kingsley lived in a separate dwelling, sharing it with her grandchild, Isabella, the daughter of her youngest son, John Maxwell, who had been in charge of Kingsley property in the Dominican Republic since 1846. Anna's residence was adjacent to that of her eldest daughter, Martha Baxter, and only four miles from the estate of her second daughter, Mary Sammis. Within walking distance were other grandchildren and great-grandchildren. After the traumas of her early life, having family nearby must have provided comfort and security during her later years.

Another mixed-race family with kinship ties to the Kingsley clan resided in the free black community on the east bank of the St. Johns River. Charles J. McNeill, Zephaniah's nephew, lived at a plantation known as Reddy's Point, which adjoined the northern property line of Martha Baxter's estate. While a child, Charles had lived at Fort George Island in the house next door to his cousins, Martha and Mary. In 1860 they were again neighbors.

Charles J. McNeill was born March 6, 1811, in Wilmington, North Carolina, the son of Martha Kingsley and Dr. Daniel McNeill. He came to Florida to live with his uncle, Zephaniah Kingsley, when he was only eight years old because it was thought that the Florida climate would be beneficial to his health. Charles is described in an 1864 census as forty-eight years old, "a cripple," only four feet, eight inches tall. A family legend claims that Charles was injured as a baby when a young slave girl dropped him on his head, allegedly causing a life-long spinal deformity. One of Charles's siblings referred in 1854 to her "brother Charlie when a child on a journey for his malady."[41]

McNeill married Elizabeth Coffee, age thirty-six, a "free coloured" person born in Florida. Charles and Elizabeth were the parents of at least nine "free coloured" children: Donald, Josiah (sometimes Josh), John, Charles, Alvin, Ellen, William, Anna, and Elizabeth. Six of the children were still living at home when a Union provost marshal conducted a census of Jacksonville in 1864: Charles, Alvin, Ellen, Willie, Anna, and Eliza, ages seventeen to four. The McNeill children were Anna Kingsley's great-nieces and -nephews by marriage.[42]

Anna McNeill Whistler, mother of the artist James Whistler, came to Reddy's Point Plantation in March 1858 to visit her brother Charles. It had been thirty years since her last visit to the South, and she was delighted by the "lovely climate" that seemed to benefit her health. On March 23 she wrote to her son James describing red birds that were cavorting in the blossoming citrus trees and the berry patches and "peach orchards blushing with promise."[43]

Although Reddy's Point was a working plantation, and demanded the full attention of her brother during the planting and harvest seasons, Anna Whistler found it a delightful place to vacation. She decided against sailing excursions during the day in order to partake of "the sea breezes on the Piazza, looking down the St. Johns two miles wide." She enjoyed dining on "oysters and fine fresh fish" but recognized the difficulty of acquiring fresh seafood during "planting season [when] the small band of field hands are in requisition, Uncle Charlie with them. When he comes in he always appears the gentleman."

Anna Whistler advised her son to "be proud of your Uncle Charlie. He is so true hearted; his only boast being that his father was an honest man!" She was pleased to learn that Charles had cultivated a "taste for literature [which] leads him to keeping up with the times and their changes, agriculture is his pursuit and he informs himself of the improvements."

The major surprise in the letter is the news it contains of an affectionate relationship between Anna Whistler's mother, Martha Kingsley McNeill, and Charles's wife and children. Anna Whistler wrote, "I really must commend the mother of his promising sons for training them so gently and firmly to do right. I have been chaplain as regularly as teacher and trust she will never omit family worship." Credit for these character traits was attributed to her mother, who had visited at Reddy's Point and trained her daughter-in-law: "My Mother's lessons are impressed on Uncle Charlie's wife. She was a poor girl and motherless, my Mother taught her and now she acquits herself neatly as a lady. The house is a log house, but neatly kept though so barely furnished."

Elizabeth Coffee McNeill was a free African American, the daughter of a white planter and a former slave. Martha Kingsley McNeill's grandchildren in Florida, like her brother Zephaniah's grandchildren, were of mixed-race parentage. Evidence of an affectionate relationship between Martha and her son's family is endearing but unexpected given her attempts to disinherit her own brother's African wives and mixed-race children and grandchildren.

The flowering vines that Anna Whistler said her mother persuaded Charles to plant indicate that Martha McNeill actually visited at Reddy's Point prior to her death on April 7, 1852, at Stonington, Connecticut. She must have known at least the older three of her nine mixed-race grandchildren. At the time she visited with Charles, her niece, Martha Kingsley Baxter, lived at the farm on the southern boundary of his Reddy's Point Plantation. Another niece, Mary Kingsley Sammis, resided just a few miles beyond. Anna Madgigine Jai Kingsley, the wife of Martha's brother, Zephaniah, lived at a small farm nearby. It is interesting to ponder whether Martha ever regretted the lawsuit she initiated to disinherit her mixed-race in-laws, or whether she ever attempted a reconciliation with Anna.[44]

Anna Kingsley and Martha McNeill were the principal antagonists in the 1846 legal challenge to Zephaniah Kingsley's will. Prior to that contest they had known each other at Fort George Island, when Martha came to visit with her son Charles. Given the stakes involved in the lawsuit, Anna's dedication to family, her keen business sense, and the racially demeaning nature of the lawsuit, it is hard to imagine her initiating a reconciliation, or that one ever occurred.

Anna Kingsley and Charles McNeill, however, had known each other in very different ways. Anna was a young mother at the time she met Charles; he was a child with a severe physical affliction living in her husband's residence. Anna watched Charles grow up at Fort George Island and become a committed husband and father to a mixed-race family. There would have been time and reason for Anna to accept Charles and Elizabeth Coffee McNeill and their children as members of the free black community north of Pottsburgh Creek.

The rural enclave inhabited by the Kingsley, Sammis, Baxter, and McNeill families, the men and women whom they liberated from slavery (with family names of Kingsley, Wright, Williams, and Phillips), and the other free black families living "Eastside of St. Johns River" (headed by Elizabeth King, Cornelia Taylor, George Hagins, and John B. Richard) constituted a unique free African American community. John Sammis, a wealthy and respected white businessman, wielded considerable influence in Jacksonville, thanks to his strong ties to the pro-Union parties of the time and to the Kingsley family's long tenure in the region. The influence and deference Sammis enjoyed provided protection for the black men and women who moved from slave to free status and who, despite its being illegal, settled in the region near their former owners. Discrimination and race hysteria intensified during the 1850s, but the free black community east of the St. Johns River escaped the excesses of the era.

It should not be forgotten, however, that the economic status of several families in this community was based on slavery. Four mixed-race families controlled much of the land and financial resources in the area during the decade of the 1850s, and their livelihoods depended heavily on slave labor. By 1860 they must have determined that the secessionist hysteria of the 1850s was heading toward disunion and war and that slave property was no longer a safe investment. When the sheriff of Duval County came to their residences in 1860, he tallied only a handful of enslaved domestic servants living in quarters where a few months before approximately 150 slaves had resided. John and Mary Sammis and Martha Baxter had converted their slave properties to cash and were making plans to move their families to the North.

After having owned more than fifty slaves in the late 1850s, Martha had sold all but four adults and eight children by 1860. Judging from the ages of the remaining adults (two males, ages eighty and twenty-eight; and two females, both twenty-seven), it appears they were domestic servants. Martha was still a wealthy woman, with real estate valued at $5,000 and a personal estate worth $52,000. She had begun investing in real estate near Jacksonville's business district and in building lots in the nearby neighborhood of La Villa.

John Sammis transported his slaves to Louisiana to sell at the New Orleans market to sugar planters still confident that slavery would last indefinitely. Many decades later an elderly woman remembered the day in early 1860 when the Sammis slaves packed their belongings and boarded a ship at the wharf on Pottsburgh Creek. Ophelia Moore had been a young enslaved woman then, but she was still alive in the 1930s and able to recall the events of that day. She remembered standing on the riverbank and watching as a ship passed by carrying the Sammis slaves (and perhaps others owned by Anna Jai Kingsley and Martha Baxter) down the St. Johns River and away from Florida.[45]

One person who was aboard that ship was still alive in 1925, and her account supports Ophelia Moore's recollection. A Jacksonville newspaper reporter came to the Arlington home of Esther Lottery in 1925, after hearing she was approximately 100 years old and a former slave. She was unable to remember her exact date of birth, but stated that she had been born at Fort George Island as the property of Zephaniah Kingsley, and had moved with her family to San Jose Plantation shortly before her owner died. She was the youngest of eight children born to Bonify and Mary Napoleon.[46]

After Zephaniah Kingsley's death in 1843, the Napoleon family was inherited by George Kingsley. The entire family was then purchased by John Sammis at the probate auction following George's death in 1846. Bonify Napoleon had worked as an apprentice to carpenter William Kingsley at San Jose Plantation before Sammis brought the entire family to his Pottsburgh Creek estate. Esther's siblings were Beck, Scipio, Louis, George, Tena, June, and Sarah. At the Sammis plantation, Esther married an enslaved man named Quash Lottery before that day in 1860 when the slaves were shipped to the New Orleans slave market. She was purchased at auction by John Pratt, the owner of a country estate at nearby Bellevue. At the end of the Civil War, Esther and Quash Lottery returned to Jacksonville to live on land deeded to them by John Sammis.[47]

Fifteen slaves worked Anna Kingsley's farm fields at Chesterfield in the 1850s, but she owned only four on April 24, 1860, when she dictated her last will and testament. Their names were Julia, Elizabeth, Joe, and Polly, and they ranged in age from nine to seventeen. Given their ages, they may have been siblings, probably domestic servants, but chattel property nevertheless. Anna's will directed that in the event of her death, these slave children were to be sold and the proceeds divided among her grandchildren. No provisions were made to reunite them with family or keep them together if they were siblings; they were to be turned into cash. When Anta Majigeen Ndiaye's history as a slave is remembered, and the tenacious way she fought to protect her own children from captivity and enslavement in 1813, it is troubling to read this section of her will. (See Appendix.)

As it worked out, Polly, Joe, Elizabeth, and Julia became free persons and citizens of the United States of America as the result of the inferno that soon inflamed the entire nation. It is probable they found freedom in the crowded port cities north of Jacksonville as Anna and her daughters fled the area to escape the wrath of vengeful Confederate neighbors. Anna Kingsley would again be in flight, this time as a woman of nearly seventy years seeking refuge in another unknown land.

8 · Final Flight
The American Civil War

BY 1860 Anna Kingsley's own traumatic experience of captivity and slavery lay a half-century in the past. A tough and courageous survivor, Anna had prospered in freedom and become the owner of land and slaves. But as she neared seventy years of age, she increasingly placed her fate in the hands of her daughters, Martha Baxter and Mary Sammis. She lived in comfortable circumstances surrounded by grandchildren and great-grandchildren in the rural free black community she had helped to create. But the anomalous position of free blacks in northeast Florida became untenable as white supremacist sentiments intensified along with secession fever. When the bonds of union were severed, the threat to Anna Kingsley's freedom and safety was as real and frightening as anything she had faced earlier in her life. In 1862 she was again forced to flee from her home, this time because of the decision by Florida's leaders to join the other southern states in seceding from the Union, an action that was soon followed by devastating civil war.

The secessionist euphoria came at a time of unparalleled economic prosperity in Florida. The rapid population growth and economic expansion that followed the Second Seminole War had led to the opening of new plantation lands to the west of Duval County.

Cotton planters and their slaves passed through the Jacksonville port on their way to what would later become Alachua and Columbia Counties. Settlers opened new communities as far south as Fort Pierce on the Atlantic Coast, and along the Manatee River on the Gulf Coast. Cotton prices were at record highs, lumber mills proliferated from Pensacola to Jacksonville, and two railroads were under construction late in the decade. Florida's population rose from 87,000 residents in 1850 to 140,000 by 1860, as cotton and lumber exports drew hopeful planters to the rural areas of the state, and northern merchants and artisans to the booming port towns.[1]

The rapid growth and expansion contributed to general economic prosperity but could not diminish a serious political crisis in the region, one linked to national debates over the extension of slavery into the western territories of the United States. Political leaders in Florida and throughout the South believed fervently that slavery and states' rights were inseparable and not subject to political compromise. "Southern rights" had come to mean the unquestioned and unrestricted right to own slave property and to move slaves into the western territories. Defense of property rights had come to mean protection of slave property from abolitionists.[2]

The national political crises of the late antebellum years intensified racial tensions in Florida. At town meetings in Jacksonville in 1850, speakers condemned members of Congress for considering the admission of California to the Union as a free state. Although Congress repealed the hated Missouri Compromise, residents of Jacksonville denounced the Compromise of 1850 as an abolitionist-inspired document and demanded that their representatives in Washington defend "Southern rights." Secede from the Union, they demanded, before the rights of slaveholders to carry human property into the western territories are compromised away. Oscar Hart, the sometimes mercurial son of town founder Isaiah D. Hart, insisted that further compromise would encourage northern abolitionists to "place about our necks the galling chains of perpetual servitude and slavery."[3]

Madison S. Perry ran a successful gubernatorial campaign in 1856 as a states' rights Democrat. John Milton won the same office in 1860 after campaigning as a pro-secession Democrat. North Florida planter and railroad owner David Levy Yulee was one of the most radical pro-secession members of the U.S. Senate. Congressional debate over admission of Kansas and Nebraska to the Union so infuriated Edward Hopkins, a Florida candidate for governor in 1860, that he announced plans to recruit a company of a hundred armed men to go to Kansas to protect the rights of the slave states.

The success of the Republican Party in the 1860 national elections was more than many Floridians would tolerate. Although President Abraham Lincoln had repeatedly pledged that he would uphold slavery under the U.S. Constitution, his firm opposition to the expansion of slavery into the territories convinced southern extremists that the president-elect was a radical abolitionist. Newspapers in the state called for resistance and secession. Governor Madison Perry, in a November 26 speech to the Florida General Assembly, said white Floridians faced grim choices: either secede or face a slave insurrection. The General Assembly authorized the election of delegates to a "People's Convention" to determine whether Florida should secede.

Upon learning of the General Assembly's action, leaders of the secessionist movement in Jacksonville staged a mass demonstration with speeches and a fifteen-gun salute. News of a unanimous pro-secession vote in the South Carolina legislature prompted wild celebrations in Jacksonville streets in late December 1860, and soon after bands of vigilantes began intimidating known Union supporters. The name "Yankee is meaner than nigger, the lowest name a person can have," the wife of merchant Calvin L. Robinson wrote; secessionists were calling "every person born north of Mason and Dixon's line by the meanest names they can command."[4]

The sheriff of Duval County, Paul B. Canova, was elected captain of the Duval Minute Men, a "semi-political, semi-military" assemblage of leading citizens who as "true sons of the South pledged to take up arms in the defense of the State, but vote for Secession, and do all in their power to promote its passage."[5] A newspaper reporter insisted that the northern states had "razed our cities to the ground, poisoned the waters of our wells, corrupted the hearts of our servants, placed murderous weapons in their hands to turn against the breasts of their masters . . . [and] stimulated insurrection."[6]

Florida's "People's Convention" began meeting on January 3, 1861. Only seven days later the delegates voted sixty-two to seven to withdraw from the Union. By February 4, Florida representatives had gathered at Montgomery, Alabama, to participate in the formation of the Confederate States of America. Only two months later, on April 12, Confederate batteries in Charleston harbor opened fire on U.S. forces at Fort Sumter. The American Civil War had begun.[7]

John Sammis returned from the "People's Convention" with growing fear for the safety of his family and property. He owned valuable real estate and a retail store on Jacksonville's Bay Street that was well stocked with goods. Sammis soon converted his human property to cash via the New Orleans slave market, but disposing of his real estate and mercantile goods proved impossible. Northern merchants and sales representatives avoided Jacksonville after Florida seceded from the Union, and northern mill owners stopped purchasing its raw materials. Sammis's prized Strawberry Mills sawmill, woodlands, and agricultural fields drew no buyers. Wealthy whites with mixed-race families, like Sammis, and affluent mixed-race heads of households, like Martha Baxter, were trapped by the same property that had provided them economic protection for decades. Unwilling to abandon their property, or to have it confiscated by Confederate authorities, yet fearful for their safety and freedom, they shuttered the windows and hoped to ride out the coming storm.[8]

The dangers, along with the economic crisis, escalated after the U.S. Navy imposed a blockade of Atlantic and Gulf ports in April 1861. A flood of rambunctious volunteers joined northeast Florida's militia companies and marched defiantly in the town streets, but store owners faced bankruptcy. Merchants with stockpiles of goods were confronted by Confederate officers who confiscated materials for the use of their regiments.

Known Union supporters in Jacksonville behaved deferentially in the months following formation of the Confederate States of America. John Sammis, with an African-American wife and numerous mixed-race children, exercised special caution. He had an extraordinary burden in dangerous times. His challenge was to find a way to protect his family and the community of free blacks who lived nearby. The Sammis and Baxter families, Anna Kingsley, and their neighbors must have met frequently to discuss strategies for survival. John L. Driggs, a nephew from New York who lived with the Sammis family for more than a decade prior to 1861, said it was unsafe to speak when Confederate supporters were nearby. Sammis confided only in family and a few trusted associates, yet he was repeatedly "threatened by anonymous letters . . . to the effect that he was known as a damned Yankee and that he had better get out of there [northeast Florida] or he would have his house burned down over his head."⁹ When he refused to subscribe to $10,000 worth of Confederate war bonds, Sammis said, "they told me they would confiscate my property and hang me."¹⁰

During the early months of the war, mandatory declarations of loyalty were debated and vigilante committees began harassing and spying on Union supporters. Free blacks were suspected of disloyalty and accused of plotting slave rebellions. Their families were threatened and the men were treated like slaves, forced to do the heavy labor required for construction of defense works along the St. Johns River. In northeast Florida, and throughout the South, free blacks feared that their liberties would be extinguished by the Confederacy. Historians Michael P. Johnson and James L. Roark have written that the free African Americans in Charleston, South Carolina, decided that "in the newly independent South they would no longer be dark-skinned free persons but would be made light-skinned slaves."¹¹

Tensions came to a violent head in the spring of 1862, when a U.S. naval expedition arrived at the mouth of the St. Johns River. The South Carolina ports of Hilton Head and Port Royal had fallen to Union forces the previous November and had subsequently become headquarters for the South Atlantic Blockading Squadron. When coaling stations for the squadron were needed farther south along the coast, the Florida towns of Fernandina, St. Augustine, and Key West were captured by a combined Union army and navy force.¹²

Federal gunboats anchored off the mouth of the St. Johns River on March 8, prompting an exodus of Confederate supporters. It would take six more days for the gunboats to reach Jacksonville, however. During the interim, a special battalion of Confederate soldiers arrived with orders to burn strategic facilities and supplies. Sawmills and stockpiles of cut lumber, foundries, and machine shops were torched by soldiers, while vandals and arsonists burned homes and businesses owned by known Union supporters.¹³

Over 400 intensely patriotic Union supporters remained in town to welcome Union troops and convince their commanders to consider a permanent occupation of the town. On March 19, 1862, General Thomas W. Sherman, senior army commander at Hilton Head, arrived in Jacksonville to investigate the feasibility of occupying the town as a base to bring Florida back into the Union. The following day loyal citizens began registering their names with the provost marshal. A public meeting of a hundred Unionists, including John S. Sammis, drew up a proclamation urging loyal Florida residents to form a new state government and rejoin the Union. General Sherman and Admiral Samuel F. Du Pont increased the occupying troop strength to sixteen companies, convinced "Florida will soon be regenerated."[14]

Less than two weeks later, the Unionists' dreams of a permanent occupation of Jacksonville were shattered. Major General David Hunter decided federal forces were overextended in the Department of the South and ordered Jacksonville evacuated. John Sammis had been so confident of a continuing Union presence that he brought fifty-five bales of cotton out of hiding and moved them to the municipal wharf. But on April 9, 1862, the Sammis family joined the lines of forlorn refugees waiting to board Union naval transports. It is believed that Anna Kingsley and Martha Baxter and her family joined the Sammises on a ship bound for Fernandina on April 10, 1862.

There is a possibility that Anna and Martha decided against evacuation, preferring instead to remain at Martha's St. Isabel Plantation. But given Martha's prominence as a wealthy free person of color during the 1840s and 1850s, and the periodic Confederate occupations of the area between 1862 and 1864, it seems unlikely the women would have felt safe at home. That option disappeared altogether on December 14, 1864, when all the dwellings and outbuildings at St. Isabel Plantation were destroyed by fire. The *Florida Union* reported the fire, noting that "only a few household effects were saved."[15] In the absence of any evidence to the contrary, it can be assumed that Anna and Martha joined the Sammis family in search of safe refuge in a northern city.

The eventual destination for the Sammis family was New York City, although there were intermediate stops and the exact route of travel cannot be traced with certainty. They may have been among the fifty Jacksonville residents who boarded the *Star of the North* at

Fernandina and steamed for New York City, or they may have gone to Hilton Head to await another transport. Former Sammis slaves and free blacks associated with Sammis testified after the war that they traveled north aboard the steamer *Cosmopolitan* for the first leg of their journey. Albert Sammis disembarked at Fernandina and worked on construction at Fort Clinch before joining his father in New York. Alonzo Williams, a former Sammis family slave, worked at Fernandina throughout the war. William Cummings said, "we all went to Beaufort, South Carolina, by the steamer *Cosmopolitan*."[16] George Napoleon, one of the sons of the carpenter Bonify Napoleon, remembered going much farther north with the Sammis family, to Philadelphia, where he joined Company D of the Twenty-fifth Pennsylvania Volunteers.

Several free blacks and slaves involved in the flight from Jacksonville joined federal regiments to fight for the Union and freedom. George Kingsley Sammis, the son of John and Mary, enlisted May 21, 1863, at Newburgh, New York, for service in Company B, Third New York Infantry. It is not known if any of his family members accompanied him to the Newburgh area. Later in the war he served in the Seventh New York Independent Battery.[17] When John Sammis journeyed from New York to Hilton Head to begin work as a member of the U.S. Direct Tax Commission of East Florida, he was accompanied by his son Albert C. Sammis. Albert later testified, "When we got to Camp Saxon near Beaufort my father put me in the service. I did not want to go but he forced me to. . . . At that time they were just making up the regiment and there [were] only about 75 men in the whole."[18]

Albert was eighteen years old when he joined Company A of the First South Carolina Loyal Volunteers. The regiment of former slaves was mustered into regular service as the Thirty-third Regiment of the U.S. Colored Troops under the command of Colonel Thomas Wentworth Higginson. Albert participated in the daring raid up the St. Marys River to King's Ferry and the Alberti plantation and sawmill that Higginson described in his book, *Army Life in a Black Regiment*. Lieutenant Albert Sammis was Higginson's orderly when the Thirty-third captured Jacksonville in 1863.

John Sammis served on the Direct Tax Commission of Florida

from August 1862 until November 1863. During those months he maintained a residence in Fernandina, although he occasionally journeyed to New York, Philadelphia, Washington, and Beaufort. It is probable that Mary Sammis and the rest of the family lived with him in Fernandina. There is evidence that Mary was in Fernandina in April 1863, when she purchased a headstone and had it inscribed and placed over the grave of her friend Theresa Acker. The Acker family had purchased land from Mary and her husband and lived in close proximity to the Sammises for several decades. Theresa died during the war and was buried at the Bosque Bello Cemetery in Fernandina.[19]

John Sammis resigned from the Direct Tax Commission in November 1863. By the end of February 1864 he was back in Jacksonville, operating his store in the Sammis Block on Bay Street. This return was made possible by the decision of Major General Quincy A. Gillmore to reoccupy Jacksonville (for the fourth time), and to renew efforts to reconstruct a loyal government in Florida. President Abraham Lincoln gave the project enthusiastic support and even sent his personal secretary, John Hay, to begin registering loyal citizens. On February 7, 1864, the first of twenty armed transports, eight supply schooners, and assorted sloops of war, armed gunboats, and tugboats arrived at the mouth of the St. Johns River carrying more than 6,000 men.[20]

Sensing this would be a permanent occupation, Sammis returned to Jacksonville accompanied by his business partner, Thomas S. Ells, to supply the quartermaster, refugees, deserters from Confederate forces, and local residents. Clerking at the store were Sammis's sons, Edward and Egbert, and nephew John L. Driggs. Sammis prospered during the ensuing months by providing supplies and information to the occupation forces.

According to Thomas Ells, Sammis was fiercely devoted to the Union. He broke down in tears after learning of the devastating Union defeat at the Battle of Olustee, and thereafter identified the trustworthy among the refugees and Confederate deserters seeking safety and work within federal lines. As the number of loyal Unionists increased, Sammis's status as a respected community leader was restored. In June 1864 he was one of six delegates from Florida to attend the Republican Party's presidential nominating convention scheduled for June 7 at Baltimore. The Florida delegation voted for Abraham Lincoln.[21]

It is not known when Anna Kingsley and the families of Mary Sammis and Martha Baxter returned to their homes on the St. Johns River. None of them are listed in the military censuses conducted in 1864 and 1865, although John Sammis and two of his sons, as well as Charles J. McNeill, his wife, Elizabeth, and six of their nine children were recorded. The census taker found the McNeills "Eastside of the St. Johns River," undoubtedly referring to his Reddy's Point Plantation. If the census taker could find their "small log cabin," as the residence was described by McNeill's sister in 1858, it seems unlikely he would have overlooked Mary Sammis in the most prominent home on that side of the river.[22]

Perhaps Mary was still at Fernandina, where federal forces had been in control since February 1862 and free African Americans were numerous and secure. She moved there with her husband when he was appointed to the Direct Tax Commission in August 1862. The town had served as a Kingsley refuge before, in 1813 and 1814 during the "Patriot" uprising. Zephaniah had owned Fernandina property for decades. It is conceivable that the Sammises, Baxters, and Anna Kingsley again sought shelter in Fernandina in 1862 and stayed there throughout the war. The provost marshal noted on the censuses of Fernandina and Amelia Island that he had not canvassed "Colored" residents of the Old Town and Engineering departments, and that there were "probably others I couldn't locate."[23]

Of the Kingsley women, it was probably Mary who returned to the St. Johns River first. Her husband was a respected Unionist with ties to the military officers in command of Jacksonville. The large Sammis home on the St. Johns River and Pottsburgh Creek escaped damage during the war; it would have been the logical postwar place of return for Mary's elderly mother and sister.

A grand homecoming celebration was held at Mary Sammis's residence in October 1865, when her son, Edward G. Sammis, came back to Jacksonville. He had been in Liverpool, England, for at least some of the war years. On September 19, 1865, the *Florida Union* announced the wedding of Edmond (actually Edward) G. Sammis to

Eliza V. Willis of Liverpool, England, at a ceremony performed at the All St.'s Church in Liverpool. An employee of Sammis and Company, Charles L. Mather, was also married that September, to Fannie M. Sasher of Plainfield, New Jersey. Both newlywed couples, "C. L. Mather and lady, E. W. Sammis and lady," arrived in Jacksonville in late October from Savannah aboard the steamer *Fountain*.[24]

The November 4, 1865, issue of the *Florida Union* contained further evidence that stability had returned to the region. There was an advertisement for John S. Sammis and Company, wholesale and retail dealers in general merchandise, and a commentary by Holmes Steele, the associate editor and a former Confederate army officer, that he had "strolled" through the "extensive store and warehouse of Messrs. Sammis and Co." and found a "large stock of goods" for retail sale to local customers and wholesale transactions with merchants in Florida's interior.

The newspaper also announced John Sammis's election to the board of trustees of the Jacksonville Institute, hailed by the editor as "A Select School in Jacksonville." Residents of the town had turned their attention from war to weddings, agriculture, business, and education. After two decades of racial hysteria and secession frenzy and four years of war, a degree of normalcy had returned to northeast Florida. The Kingsley, Sammis, Baxter, and McNeill families, former slaves, and the free blacks who had lived in the rural community east of the St. Johns River returned to what remained of their homes.

9 · Final Years

AFTER THE CIVIL WAR, Anna Kingsley and her daughters never regained the wealth and power they had enjoyed during the antebellum years. John S. Sammis and Oran B. Baxter had migrated to Florida around 1830 with only minimal financial resources, but they became major land and slave owners soon after marrying Mary and Martha Kingsley. In 1865 slave owning as a route to wealth had finally come to an end in the United States.

Anna Kingsley, for a time a slave herself, had gained her wealth through the ownership of slaves. Her fortune had dwindled by 1860; what remained was wiped out by the war. From 1865 until her death, probably in 1870, Anna Kingsley resided with one of her daughters, bereft of resources save a loving family.

In 1860 John Sammis had possessed real and personal property worth $120,000, a sum comparable to nearly $4 million in today's currency.[1] He sold most of his human property that same year, and advertised his most valuable real estate for sale; but events moved so quickly that he had to resort to a clever dodge to prevent it from being confiscated. In June 1861, for a fee of $1, Sammis deeded Strawberry Mills and his plantation lands to a sympathetic friend, Mrs. Margaret J. Mosely. In the final months of the war the provost marshal in Jacksonville acknowledged a deed from Mosely conveying the property back to Sammis. In 1873 the heirs of Margaret Mosely issued a quit-claim deed to eliminate any possible uncertainty over the title. A note on the deed stated, "Sammis maintained uninterrupted possession."[2] Confederate authorities nevertheless confiscated more than $75,000 worth of mercantile stock and other property that Sammis never recovered, and he supplied additional merchandise to federal authorities for which he was not fully compensated. The abundant cash resources he possessed in 1860 had vanished by 1865.

Sammis sold his prized plantation in February 1866 to Daniel Dustin Hanson, William W. Marple, and Levi Markley, all Union Army officers who had come to Jacksonville during the war. Hanson was the surgeon for the Thirty-fourth Regiment of the U.S. Colored Infantry, which occupied the town in 1865 and early 1866. Prior to purchasing the Sammis property, Hanson acquired property bordering the town of Jacksonville on the north and sold it in small plots to the black soldiers of his regiment. This neighborhood of black homeowners and small farmers came to be known as Hanson Town; today it is the site of the downtown campus of the Florida State College at Jacksonville. Hanson and the black farmers joined together to purchase supplies and market crops cooperatively, hoping for greater profits than a single farmer could achieve.[3]

The Hanson Town agricultural project succeeded at first, prompting Daniel Hanson to expand the cooperative venture across the St. Johns River to plantation lands he bought from John Sammis for $14,000. Considering that real estate prices were generally depressed in the immediate postwar years, Sammis managed to sell the land for a handsome price. Hanson was optimistic enough to purchase his partners' interests, but within a year the army surgeon was dead of complications of malarial fever. Sammis foreclosed on the property and resold it in March 1871 to Lewis I. Fleming and J. J. Daniel for $8,000. Fleming and Daniel operated the sawmill for another decade.[4]

Sammis exempted from sale the hundred acres surrounding his homesite, which by then had acquired the name Arlington. Also withheld were several parcels deeded to Sammis children and to former slaves of the family. The free black community that had formed in this area prior to 1861 and been driven from the region by the war had reassembled after 1865 and been augmented by several families of former slaves.

Mary and John Sammis deeded tracts varying in size from six to ninety-nine acres to their sons Egbert C., Edward G., George Kingsley, and James Gallison Sammis. Additional tracts were deeded to John L. Driggs and Edmund C. Koppel. Driggs was a nephew and Coppel a grandson, the child of Martha Sammis Coppel. Ten acres went to Albert C. Sammis, and another thirty-eight to Antoinette Paine, Albert's mother. Albert C. Sammis, Jr., was given ninety-six acres. Mary Sammis Houston and her children, Zephaniah Kingsley, Georgiana, Henry Farrar, Louisa, Anne, and William Greenwood, still held twenty acres of land given to her by her parents in 1856.[5]

Several former slaves can be identified as landholders in the area. Quash Lottery and his wife, Esther, the daughter of carpenter Bonify Napoleon, lived at the juncture of Pottsburgh and Silversmith Creeks. Esther had returned from New Orleans after the Civil War, her passage paid by her former owner to thank her for securing valuable family possessions from marauding Union troops. John and Mary Sammis gave five acres to "Bonafy Napoleon during his life, then to George Gaston and his heirs" in gratitude for "past services." (George was Napoleon's son; after the war and Union service, he chose the surname Gaston.) Lindo Wright, freed by Anna Kingsley in the 1850s, acquired twenty acres of the Branchester tract from Sammis; in 1878 Sammis agreed to act as trustee for Lindo's surviving heirs: Sophey, Labo, Joseph, and Elizabeth.

Three miles to the north of the Branchester property, Alonzo Phillips purchased fifteen acres from Martha Baxter in 1869. Alonzo was the slave son of the carpenter William Kingsley who was purchased by his father at auction in 1848 and freed. After his father's death, Alonzo was adopted by John Sammis and became a clerk in the latter's Jacksonville store. He was a commissary sergeant in Company A, Twenty-first U. S. Colored Infantry during three years of service in the Union Army. In 1921 Phillips was still living on that fifteen-acre tract, although the area had by then acquired the name of Chaseville.[6]

At the northern edge of this free black community, Charles J. McNeill returned to live at Reddy's Point Plantation in the latter months of the war. Anna McNeill Whistler wrote that her brother's entire family was "banished" from their home "at Ready's [*sic*] Point on the St. Johns River" by the war, probably at the time Union forces evacuated in 1862.[7] After Union forces reoccupied Jacksonville in February 1864, the McNeill family returned to Reddy's Point. A census conducted later that year by the provost marshal listed McNeill and his free "coloured" wife, Elizabeth, living on the east side of the St. Johns River, along with their young children. Their son Charles, age seventeen, was living in Jacksonville and working as a Union government employee in 1864 and 1865. Donald C. McNeill, the eldest child in the family, left Jacksonville in 1861 to live with his aunt, Anna McNeill Whistler, in Philadelphia.

In August 1867, Anna Whistler reported that Donald had just arrived in Philadelphia for a visit after a six-month stay with his parents in Florida. He had been "helping his father plant orange trees, grapevines, etc. . . . just when he was most needed; for his father was about moving out of the Negro house he and his wife and six children had been obliged to live in when the one they were in was burned. So Don with his strong and willing arm got them settled again in their own [home]."[8] Donald was working at the time for the Pacific Steam Train Company in New York. His job as engineer paid $100 a month, from which he helped pay the boarding expenses of his brother Charles, who was then "in the novelty work in New York."[9]

In April 1869, before the restoration of their home was completed, Charles McNeill died. Anna Whistler wrote of her brother's "sudden death" and his "life of cheerful resignation." She added, "A great responsibility devolves on his eldest of nine children. Donald will be a great comfort to his widowed Mother. His next brother Charlie in New York is exemplary too, they both attended the funeral of their father in Stonington [Connecticut]."[10]

Little is known about Charles J. McNeill beyond his physical affliction and association with Zephaniah Kingsley, his marriage to Elizabeth Coffee, and their family life at Reddy's Point. The following excerpt from his last will and testament conveys something of his character.

> To my wife Elizabeth and my children I give and bequeath all my Estate real and personal. So long as my wife remains single and during her life, and till the youngest child shall be of age, I desire said Estate to be kept together for the use and support of all, the Farm being kept

for a homestead, and all money invested in stocks is to remain so, the interest being for the support of all alike. But should my wife marry again, then an equal share of the yearly income is to be paid her, yearly, during life, and the sum of $200 to be paid on her marriage to assist with her new household—and my sincere pray[er] is for her happiness. I desire that all my children be allowed every chance to obtain a good plain English education and when sixteen years of age, to be bound to some good trade such as they may select; should some prefer to be Farmers, which I earnestly desire and advise, as being the best and most independent mode of life, that their wishes be provided in any way as seems best to their mother and my executors. I desire my books to be kept together at the Homestead for the use of all, never to be sold or abused, my tools to be given to the son having the most love and use for them. My watch to be given to my eldest son, Donald, hoping he will value it and remember the value of time as often as he looks at it. All other articles to be divided as my wife sees best.[11]

Charles J. McNeill prepared his will on February 1, 1861, during a time of great tension and danger for a Union supporter and his mixed-race wife and children. Missing from the bequests are slave properties; Charles had owned human chattel in the past but appears to have either emancipated or sold them by 1861. Between the time the will was written and his death, the value of McNeill's estate was diminished by the ravages of war. Fire destroyed the family dwelling, and possibly consumed the books McNeill cherished and wanted preserved. His money had vanished during the war, and proceeds from the farm were not sufficient to provide shares to the children and Elizabeth. The estate could not have provided a $200 bequest to "assist with her new household" if the widow remarried. Elizabeth could carry from Reddy's Point one thought to cherish throughout her life—the memory of Charles's sincere prayer for her happiness.

The Reddy's Point Plantation was sold at probate auction to John S. Sammis. It is not clear whether McNeill's widow, Elizabeth, remained in Connecticut after his funeral, or whether she returned to Florida. Her youngest child, Alvan C. McNeill, born in 1852, remained in the Arlington neighborhood where so many Kingsley and Sammis descendants settled before and after the Civil War. In 1881 Alvan and Louisa Christensen McNeill purchased twenty acres of the

Branchester tract. Some of their descendants may still live in Jacksonville.[12]

The postwar years were difficult for everyone in the Kingsley, Sammis, Baxter, and McNeill families. John Sammis never recovered financially from the events of 1861–65. He returned to the mercantile trade after Union forces occupied Jacksonville in 1864 and appears to have restored the Sammis Building and Wharf on Bay Street. Advertisements for John S. Sammis and Company ran in Jacksonville's *Florida Times* throughout 1865 and 1866. In 1866 local alderman A. A. Canova worked as a clerk in the store. Sammis again became prominent in the Solomon Lodge of the Masonic Order, and he was elected chairman of the board of directors of the Jacksonville Gas Light Company.[13]

In 1870 Sammis reported a combined real and personal estate worth only $4,000, more than most persons in the county could report but still a shocking decline from his reported wealth of $120,000 just ten years earlier. Sammis and his wife, Mary, were living in Mandarin when the census taker called in 1870. He was no longer a wealthy businessman and planter; his occupation that year was listed as carpenter. His son Edward, a retail grocer, reported a personal estate worth $1,000. Only a few years later, Edward was working as a barber. James Gallison and Albert C. Sammis were both working as policemen in Jacksonville during the 1880s.[14]

In 1867 the Sammis family gathered for the first of many burials after the war. Interred on February 24 of that year was Selena M. Sammis, the wife of George Kingsley Sammis. George had married Selena Mooney after returning to Arlington following his service in the Union army. A tombstone in the Sammis family cemetery indicates that Selena was only twenty-eight years old at the time of her death. On six more occasions over the next four years the Baxter, Kingsley, and Sammis families would grieve the loss of a loved one at the Sammis family burial ground known today as Clifton Cemetery.[15]

The second funeral was for Martha R. Sammis, age twenty-nine, a daughter of John and Mary. A tombstone in the Sammis cemetery records Martha's date of death as December 1, 1869. Shortly before the war, Martha must have married a man named Koppell, for when Anna Kingsley composed her will in April 1860 she mentioned

"Martha Sammis, now Martha Koppell." In 1870, one year after Martha's death, a nine-year-old boy named Edward C. Koppell was living with Mary and John Sammis.

The families gathered next for the burial of Emile V. Sammis, who died February 16, 1870. Emile, the son of Mary and John Sammis, was recorded on the 1850 census as Emelia Sammis, age one, and in 1860 as Amelia B., age eleven. The child's age had been recorded accurately even if the gender and name were confused.

Eliza Willis Sammis (also known as Lizzie and Elizabeth), the English-born wife of Emile's older brother Edward G. Sammis, was the next family member to die. Married in Liverpool, Edward and Liza had moved to Jacksonville in 1865, after the war ended. In 1869 their daughter, Mary M., was born. When the 1870 census was taken, Edward was thirty-three years old, Elizabeth twenty-eight, and Mary eight months. The census taker listed Mary as a white child born in England. Within one year this Sammis grandchild would be without a mother: Liza died August 25, 1871, and was interred in the Sammis cemetery in a double burial. The top of the headstone is engraved with the words "Lizzie W. Sammis," and the bottom with "Our Dear Maud." Apparently, Liza Willis Sammis died shortly after giving birth to her second daughter, and the infant died soon after. The Sammis family lost Selena, Liza, Maud, Martha, and Emile in only four years.

These were cruel times for the Baxter family as well. Since her daughters were all married and her son was in his twenties after the war, Martha's burdens may have been lessened by not having to care for children. After returning to Duval County, she may have taken temporary shelter with her sister, Mary, at the Sammis estate until the residential complex at St. Isabel Plantation was rebuilt.[16]

Martha Kingsley had reared six children, five of whom were still alive in 1860: Anna B., twenty-six; Isabella, twenty-four; Emma Jane, twenty-two; Osmond, eighteen; and Julia Catherine, sixteen. Another daughter, also named Julia Catherine, died much earlier, on November 17, 1841, at age six. She was the first of the Baxter family to be buried at the Sammis cemetery.

Sometime between 1860 and 1870 another Baxter daughter died. Emma Jane Baxter Mocs, the wife of Joseph Mocs and mother of Belle Baxter and Emma Beatrice Mocs, died sometime during the decade.

Neither the date of her death nor the place of interment have been determined. That she died prior to February 1870 is documented in Duval County probate records.[17]

After witnessing the deaths of her husband and two daughters, Martha B. Kingsley Baxter died at her St. Isabel Plantation home on February 14, 1870. Early that day she had dictated her will in front of four witnesses. Martha was interred in the Sammis cemetery in an unmarked grave. The four-sided monument commemorating Oran B. and Julia Catherine Baxter may have been intended for Martha as well, but her name is not inscribed on the granite marker.[18]

Four months later, Anna Kingsley was dead. No public record or family legend documents the date of death; no headstone marks the place of burial. What is known is that Anna died sometime prior to June 18, 1870, the day Martha Baxter's four children delivered their grandmother's will, signed in 1860, to the Duval County Court of Probate.

Based on the documentation that remains in the probate file, it appears the Baxter siblings were engaged in the normal processes of settling the financial affairs of their mother's estate when Anna Kingsley passed away. They informed the authorities and delivered the will that Anna Kingsley had dictated in 1860. The will could have been found in either Anna's or Martha's personal papers.[19]

The evidence, however, is so minimal that the circumstances of death can be interpreted in other ways. Perhaps as Martha Baxter's children inventoried and allocated their mother's possessions and sifted through her papers, they discovered the last will and testament of a grandmother who died prior to 1870. During these times of disrupted lives and governments, with families fleeing to unknown places of refuge, the death of an elderly mother could have gone unrecorded except in the memories of her children and grandchildren. Given the turmoil of the 1860s, the years of exile, the burned-out homes, and the sickness and death that plagued the Baxters and Sammises, reporting the death of Anna Kingsley at the time it occurred may have been impossible.

The slender probate record opened by the court in June 1870 (whether the date of death was 1860 or 1870, or sometime in between) indicates that Anna Kingsley had neither assets nor debts to report.

She lived out her final days without financial resources. The will the Baxter children delivered had been written a decade earlier, at a time when Anna still possessed considerable cash assets and four enslaved human beings. These assets had all vanished by 1870.

The precise date of Anna Kingsley's death cannot be documented, but there is evidence that she was interred in an unmarked grave in the Sammis family cemetery. Although Mary and John Sammis were recorded by the 1870 census as living in the Mandarin section in Duval County, they retained the hundred acres surrounding their residence in Arlington until April 11, 1873, when the property was sold to the Florida Winter Home Association for $10,000. Even after the sale, however, Sammis family burials continued in the cemetery until at least 1895. John Sammis died in 1883 and Mary Sammis in 1895; both were interred in the family cemetery in unmarked graves. Before he died, John formally purchased the burial lot where a tombstone was placed to commemorate his daughter-in-law, Lizzie Sammis.[20]

Evidence for Anna Kingsley's burial in the Clifton Cemetery is found in the papers of the late Phil May, Sr., a prominent Jacksonville attorney and avocational historian who researched the life of Zephaniah Kingsley with care and skill. Early in 1940, May met with James N. Wilson, a teacher in Jacksonville who was related to former slaves of John Sammis and a close friend of Egbert C. Sammis. Egbert was the only child of John and Mary Sammis still alive in 1940. A former member of the Florida State Senate, one of only four black men elected to the state legislature in 1884, Egbert lived mainly in Washington after his term of elective office ended. He also briefly served as U.S. consul in Stuttgart, Germany.[21]

After several unsuccessful efforts to contact Egbert for information about his parents and grandparents, May decided to visit the Sammis family cemetery. James Wilson arranged for a knowledgeable guide: his elderly uncle, Augustus Harvey, a former slave of John Sammis. Harvey had already placed temporary identification cards over each unmarked grave by the time May arrived.

Harvey knew the history of the cemetery and its occupants exceedingly well. His deceased sister, Mollie Harvey, had also been a Sammis family slave for three decades. A house servant for Mary Sammis, Mollie was given land by the Sammis family after the Civil

War. Harvey had buried Mollie alongside the Sammises under a tombstone engraved "Aunt Mollie Harvey. Died February 23, 1904. Age 72 years 6 months."[22]

May walked with Wilson and Harvey one day in April 1940, noting the placement of graves and name markers, and writing down Harvey's comments about the Sammis family. One entry reads: "Antoinette Payne—mistress. Son: A. C. Sammis, Constable here. Alonzo Phillips—adopted son of Sammis—died recently." These and other comments May recorded can be corroborated by documented evidence.

Throughout his notes, May used sensible and clear abbreviations to record what he heard and observed. He recorded the engravings on the tombstones for Emile, Martha, Selena, and Lizzie Sammis, Aunt Mollie Harvey, Oran Baxter, and Julia C. Baxter. Then he started at the tombstone of Emile Sammis and wrote in his notes the names of persons interred in several unmarked graves to its left: "Eddie Cappel, son of Martha K. Sammis, to left of Emile. John S. [indicating John Sammis] to left; Mary K S [indicating Mary Kingsley Sammis] next to left." At this point in his notes, May interjected commentary on the backgrounds of Oran Baxter and John Sammis and the locations of

18. The home of Mary and John Sammis, in Jacksonville's Clifton area of Arlington, was built in the 1850s, perhaps by slave carpenters from East Africa. The Sammis family burial ground, now Clifton Cemetery, is located behind the dwelling. Photo by Joan E. Moore, December 1999.

19. (*left*) Headstone for Lizzie (Eliza) Willis Sammis and her infant daughter Maud in Clifton Cemetery. Born in Liverpool, England, Eliza married Edward G. Sammis, Anna Kingsley's grandson. The couple's older daughter, Mary, became the wife of A. L. Lewis, founder of the Afro-American Life Insurance Company.

20. (*right*) Grave marker at Clifton Cemetery for Emile V. Sammis, grandson of Anna Madgigine Jai Kingsley. Her own unmarked grave is to the right of the headstone for Emile. Photographs by Joan E. Moore, April 2002.

their Duval County properties. Only then did he identify the gravesite of Anna Kingsley. May's note reads: "a. Rt. Mother. Hannah princess. Knew Kingsley." Like many transcribers who heard blacks pronounce Anna Kingsley's given name, May wrote down Hannah rather than Anna. August Harvey, a former slave who had known both Mary K. Sammis and her African mother, told May that Anna Kingsley, once an African princess who knew Zephaniah Kingsley, was buried at the right of Emile V. Sammis's grave.

At least this much is certain. Anta Majigeen Ndiaye, the Wolof princess from Senegal who became Anna Madgigine Jai Kingsley in Florida, was buried in a peaceful grove near the St. Johns River. Her final resting place is surrounded by the graves of her daughters and the other family members she loved in life. She rests in peaceful repose in an unmarked grave sheltered from the violence and trauma that followed her through a life marked by danger, courage, tenacious defense of family, flight, and triumphant return.

A Personal Postscript

FOR MORE THAN a quarter century I have visited the Sammis family burial ground to walk amid the head-stones and ponder the Kingsley legacy. The Clifton Cemetery, as it is now known, is the final resting place of Anta Majigeen Ndiaye, her daughters, and many of her grandchildren. It is respectfully maintained by vol-unteer members of the Arlington Garden Club, but no headstones mark the graves of Anna and her daugh-ters. A historical marker erected by Old Arlington Inc., now stands by the cemetery to inform passersby of the meaningful lives that were led by Anna Kingsley, Martha Baxter, and Mary Sammis. Their unique role in the history of northeast Florida, and in the creation of the black community that once existed in what is today the Arlington area of Jacksonville, is worthy of commemoration.

I have often been drawn to the place where Anna's spirit is most acutely felt, Kingsley Plantation at Fort George Island. Anna lived at Fort George Island in se-curity and comfort for more than two decades, longer than at any other location. The "Ma'am Anna House," built for her after the "Patriot War" of 1812–15, still stands beside the residence of Zephaniah Kingsley. Across from the "Ma'am Anna House" are the well, carriage house, and stable that were constructed when the Kingsley family owned the island. The graceful avenue of cedars that Anna viewed from her front windows provides needed shade for the thousands of visitors who walk the grounds each year and view the buildings maintained by the National Park Service.

One day soon these dwellings will be renovated, appropriately furnished, and fully opened for inspection. Visitors will then be able to view the kitchen and oversized fireplace in the "Ma'am Anna" house where food was prepared for guests in the main dwelling. The sitting room where Anna entertained Susan Philippa Fatio L'Engle on Sunday afternoons will serve as a reminder that white and black women born on different continents could become respectful friends in a Florida dominated by slavery and racial prejudice.

Research in 1999 by Carol Davis Clark, a park ranger at the Timucuan Ecological and Historic Preserve, has provided knowledge of the flowers, trees, and other plants Anna cultivated around her house. Just south of her dwelling, beyond banana trees and a well and windmill, stood an aviary where Anna tended ducks and geese, as she had at her homestead in Mandarin before it was destroyed during the Patriot Rebellion. At the rear of her dwelling she viewed ornamental vegetation surrounding a plantation cemetery. During the 1870s the cemetery disappeared from view when a new owner detached the headstones and covered them with dirt. The identity of the inhabitants of the invisible graves will not be known until the cemetery is restored to its original state.[1]

A long stretch of sparsely wooded land separates the Anna and Zephaniah houses from the remains of the tabby cabins that once housed their slave laborers. This space was once filled with fruit trees and the personal gardens of the slaves. The wells that supplied fresh water have been filled; the fig trees that bloomed in front of the dwellings have vanished. Only one of the slave cabins on the semicircular arc of dwellings has been restored to its former appearance, but the foundations and lower exterior walls of most of the other cabins remain. During the decades after Anna Kingsley departed Fort George Island, roots and vines—abetted by heat and rain, freezes, and vandals—destroyed the roofs and the upper portions of the walls of some of the tabby cabins. The dwellings stand diminished but expressive of the spirit of their former occupants, whose lives remain unrecorded. Fortunately, National Park Service plans for Kingsley Planta-

21. The avenue of palms Anna and Mary Kingsley planted at Fort George Island in the early 1830s still thrives. Offshoots from the original plantings continue to grow into mature trees. Photograph by Joan E. Moore, April 2002.

tion give high priority to interpreting the slaves' lives. Visitors will learn about the music, dance, art, culinary habits, and other cultural practices of the men and women who once lived in these tabby dwellings.

A walk along the road leading south and away from the slave quarters and toward the entrance to Fort George Island evokes strong memories of Anna Kingsley. More than a half-century after marrying and moving away from Fort George Island, Mary Kingsley Sammis remembered that road in an interview with William Hawley. She told of helping her mother plant the palm trees that formed the storied entrance to Kingsley Plantation's residential complex. Palms line that drive today—not the original plants set out under the direction of Anna Kingsley, but plucky offshoots that still lead visitors to her homesite.

National Park Service rangers lead thousands of tourists from many nations through the "Ma'am Anna" and "Zephaniah" houses every year. Among the visitors have been descendants of Anna and Zephaniah who traveled from the Dominican Republic to learn more about the history of their ancestors. I have met many of the descendants—in the Dominican Republic and at Kingsley Plantation—and have been greatly enriched by the experience. It is the dream of one of those descendants, Manuel Lebrón, to establish a second memorial to Anna and Zephaniah, a Kingsley museum at Cabaret Village on the north shore of the Dominican Republic, near the site where Anna Madgigine Jai Kingsley walked the beach wearing replicas of the African gowns she remembered from her childhood in Senegal. Manuel and his parents, Sandra and Tony Lebrón, walked with me along Cabaret Harbor in 1994 and in 1995, after guiding me through interviews with other Kingsley descendants in the Dominican Republic. Generous and thoughtful people, they are proud of their ancestral link to Anta Majigeen Ndiaye. I hope once again to walk along that beach with the Lebrón family, and to visit the Kingsley Museum after Manuel's dream becomes reality.

In March 2000, on a spot overlooking a beach on the African side of the Atlantic Ocean, a memorial of another sort was held at Gorée Island, Senegal, to honor Anna Kingsley. At the very place from which the teenage captive named Anta Majigeen Ndiaye was sold to a slave ship's captain and transported to the Americas, a historical conference marked the return of her indomitable spirit to her African homeland. The memory of Anta Majigeen Ndiaye, torn away from home and family when she was only thirteen years old, was embraced in the nation of Senegal, where Wolof culture and history still thrive.

The conference had its origin in 1998, when Jennifer Chase, a University of North Florida student and Rotary International Ambassadorial Student, joined with African musicians in Dakar, Senegal, to record a song honoring Anna Kingsley. The recording, titled "Anta Majigeen Ndiaye," became popular on Senegalese radio and television. Subsequent support from the Florida Division of Cultural Affairs, the Florida Humanities Council, and individuals and departments at the University of North Florida led to the Anna Kingsley in Senegal Historical Conference at Gorée Island in March 2000. Professor Mbaye Guèye, dean of Liberal Arts and Sciences at Cheikh Anta Diop University, gave able direction to an event that had been encouraged by the Honorable Abdou Diouf, who retired in April 2000 after twenty years as President of Senegal.[2] Before the election in April 2000 that led to his retirement, President Diouf had arranged a visit to the "Ma'am Anna House" at Kingsley Plantation. His goal was to pay tribute to Anta Majigeen Ndiaye with a presidential entourage of Wolof dancers and singers. Because of the election results, the visit was canceled.

It was my good fortune to participate in that conference, and to travel to the site of Yang Yang, the ancient capital of Jolof where it is believed that Anta's youth ended tragically on the day in 1806 when she became a captive of tyeddo warriors. Joined by my wife, Joan Moore, and Dr. Jane Landers of Vanderbilt University, I met with a Wolof historian and the elders of the village of Yang Yang, once the home of kings of Jolof, and with government officials at the nearby regional town of Dahra, Jolof. Those poignant experiences have enhanced my understanding of Anna Kingsley's African origins and cultural background and her place in the New World diaspora of Wolof women.

Finally, during the research and writing of this book, I was reminded of how little we know about the African heritage of the black men and women who lived as slaves in northeast Florida. Personal

22. María Abedona Pérez Kingsley, the great-granddaughter of Anna Kingsley through her youngest son, John Maxwell. Photo courtesy of Sandra Lebrón, María's granddaughter.

23. Sandra Lebrón, a great-great-great granddaughter of Anna Kingsley, and her son Manuel at their home in Santo Domingo, Dominican Republic. Photo by the author.

letters and diaries cannot be found. I have not been able to locate a portrait or photograph of Anna or Zephaniah Kingsley, or of their children. That is why I am deeply thankful to the staff at Kingsley Plantation for preserving a photograph of "Aunt Easter" (Esther Bartley), the daughter of Bonify Napoleon, the carpenter from East Africa who once lived in the slave quarters at the Sammis plantation.

One day I may travel to Kibuezi, a Kamba village in southern Tanzania where the carpenter William Kingsley and his apprentice, Bonify Napoleon, are believed to have practiced the craft of woodcarving until the awful day in 1805 when raiders captured them and marched them to a slave market in Mozambique. By 1806 they had been purchased by Zephaniah Kingsley, carried across the Atlantic in the cargo space of his ship, the *Gustavia,* and put to work as carpenters at Laurel Grove Plantation. William Kingsley was eventually freed, and Bonify Napoleon became the slave of Mary and John Sammis.

When the home of John and Mary Sammis was built in the 1850s, there is reason to believe these two black carpenters were among the

24. Esther Bartley, also "Aunt Easter," born a slave at Kingsley Plantation, the daughter of Bonify Napoleon, a slave carpenter. John Sammis purchased the Napoleon family at auction. Photo courtesy of the National Park Service, Timucuan Ecological and Historic Preserve.

craftsmen who did the work. Each time I drive by the Sammis residence, a National Register of Historic Places site in Jacksonville's Clifton subdivision, I think about William Kingsley and Bonify Napoleon, about their skill as carpenters and the way they survived slavery. Captured in slaving wars in East Africa, they became honorable family men in Florida whose sons fought in regiments of the Colored Infantry in order to end slavery in the United States.

If there are descendants of Mary Sammis who drive by the house, one wishes they could come to know the African songs and stories Mary heard from her mother. Anta Majigeen Ndiaye, the thirteen-year-old Wolof girl who became Anna Madgigine Jai Kingsley in Florida, would surely have carried with her to the Americas a portion of the rich cultural tradition of the Wolof people of Senegal.

Appendix

The Last Will and Testament
of Anna Madgigine Jai Kingsley

KNOW ALL MEN BY THESE PRESENTS, that I Anna M. Kingsley of the County of Duval and State of Florida being of sound mind and memory but feeble in strength, do hereby, and by these presents constitute and appoint my daughter Martha B. Baxter my true and lawful attorney in fact and trustee to act for me in all my business and to hold in trust all my property and effects of every kind whatsoever, as if I had it in my possession and acted in person myself during the balance of my natural life. And I have and do hereby place in her hands and put her in the full and undisturbed possession of the following amount of money and possessions—viz: Three Thousand dollars in cash and four Negro Slaves viz: Polly a woman aged about (17) seventeen years- Joe a boy about (14) fourteen, Elizabeth a girl about (12) twelve and Julia a girl about (9) nine years. Also all my right title and interest in and to a certain claim I have as one of the legatees of and under the will of Zephaniah Kingsley late of East Florida in which he the said Kingsley bequeaths and devises to me, one twelfth part of any amount or sum of money that shall be allowed him or his heirs by the government of the United States for losses sustained by him during the War of 1812 and 1813 by the operations of the American Army, the principal having been allowed, the interest money is now pending before the Congress of the U. States.

I do hereby clothe my said attorney to use all due diligence in legally prosecuting the collection of said claim, to sue and be sued as if by me in person, and to employ such aid as she may deem proper, and if said claims are allowed, to collect and receive the same. The whole of the above described money, property and claims is nevertheless in trust for my use and benefit and the educating and other necessary expenses of my granddaughter Isabella B. Kingsley, during my lifetime. My said attorney having the full power to loan out the money, sell the slaves whenever she may see fit to do so, convey title to same, all of which shall be binding on me and my heirs forever.

And at my death I wish the trust and ownership to continue the same as before, and I do hereby continue the same as a part of my last will and testament as follows viz: I wish my daughter Martha B. Baxter to defray all my funeral expenses, and pay all my just debts, and divide the three thousand dollars aforesaid or so much thereof as she may have left in her hands after the completion of my said granddaughter's education, between the children of my son John Maxwell Kingsley of San Domingo, just as she may see fit and proper, and in such sums and at such times as she may select, having the utmost confidence in her good judgement to act for them. And the money she may receive for the two negro slaves, aforesaid Elizabeth and Julia, I wish her to give (without any interest thereon) to my daughter Mary K. Sammis. But with the express understanding that she Mary K. shall give the same to her children equally divided, at such time as she may deem well and proper.

The Interest money aforesaid I wish my daughter Martha to divide equally between her own daughters and the daughter of Mary K. Sammis now Martha Koppel if she be living, and if not to divide the same between her own daughters aforesaid.

I wish my daughter Martha B. Baxter to receive the interest money directly from *the government* if it is allowed and defray all the expenses of collecting out of the same.

The residue of all my estate of every kind whatsoever, including the proceeds of the sale of the two slaves aforesaid Polly and Joe, and all that she may discover in any manner belonging to me either real or personal I do hereby give and bequeath to my beloved daughter Martha to have and to hold forever in fee.

I wish my daughter Martha B. and I do hereby invest in her full power to act as my trustee and Executrix to this my last will without entering into or giving bond or security for her faithful performance as I have the most implicit confidence in her, and wish her to act, no matter where I may live or die and without any regard to her own residence no matter whether in or out of the United States. I don't want any one to have anything to do with what I may leave, except Martha B. Baxter for many reasons, one of which is to prevent lawsuits, and if anyone shall attempt either in person or by agent to disturb this my last will, I wish my daughter Martha to withhold from them all participation in my effects.

Given from under my hand and seal this [24th] day of April, one thousand and eight hundred and sixty, in presence of the subscribing witnesses. I do hereby fully authorize and invest my said attorney trustee and Executrix to employ such aid as she may deem necessary to assist her during my lifetime and defray all the necessary expenses of the same, out of the money she may have on hand belonging to me and after my death if she deems it necessary to employ aid, she is fully authorized to do so, and also to appoint a successor at her death to carry out the provisions of the foregoing trust and will, just as if she were doing it for herself, and to defray all the expenses of the same out of any money she may have on hand belonging to my estate.

I do hereby appoint my daughter Martha B. Baxter my Executrix to this my last will and testament and I hereby annul and revoke all other powers of attorney, trusts or wills, heretofore made by me.

Given under my hand and seal this twenty fourth day of April, one thousand eight hundred and sixty.

Anna M. Kingsley (Seal)
Artemesia Curtiss
Ann Jane Whittlesey
Charlotte Joyner
Stephen M. Joyner [witnesses]

Notes

Abbreviations

BIFAN   *Bulletin de l'Institute Fondamental d'Afrique Noir*. Universitaire Cheikh Anta Diop, Dakar, Sénégal.

CO   Colonial Office Papers. PRO.

EFP   East Florida Papers Manuscript Collection, Library of Congress.

FSA   Florida State Archives. Bureau of Archives and Records Management, Department of State, Division of Library and Information Services, R. A. Gray Building, Tallahassee.

JHSL   Jacksonville Historical Society Library. Jacksonville University Library, Jacksonville.

JML   Jacksonville Main Library, Florida and Genealogy Room, Jacksonville Public Libraries.

NA   National Archives of the United States. Washington, D.C.

PKY   P.K. Yonge Library of Florida History, University of Florida Libraries, Gainesville.

PRO   Public Record Office, Great Britain, Kew, Surrey, England.

PWC   Patriot War Papers and Patriot War Claims, 1812-1846. SAHSRL.

SAHSRL   St. Augustine Historical Society Research Library, St. Augustine.

Preface

1. Corse, *Key to the Golden Islands*, 115–16.
2. Mills, *Letters from New-York*, 98.
3. Benjamin, "The Sea Islands," 844.
4. L'Engle, *The Summer of the Great-Grandmother*, 187–88. I thank Catherine Strayer for bringing the story and book to my attention and Carol Clark for a special gift of the book.
5. Quote is from Corse, *Key to the Golden Islands*, 133.
6. Ibid., 116.
7. For "Anna Jai," I did the research and Michael Nyenhuis the reporting. I

was the sole author of the two editions of *Anna Kingsley* and of "Shades of Freedom: Anna Kingsley in Senegal, Florida and Haiti."

8. The authors I relied on are Berlin, *Slaves without Masters*; Curry, *The Free Black in Urban America*; Degler, *Neither Black nor White*; Hogan and Davis, *William Johnson's Natchez*; Johnson and Roark, *Black Masters* and *No Chariot Let Down*; Koger, *Black Slaveowners*; Wikramanayake, *A World in Shadow*; and Williamson, *New People*.

Introduction

1. Deed of emancipation, East Florida Papers, reel 172, bundle 376 (EFP R172 B376 hereafter).

2. The copy of Zephaniah Kingsley's will in his probate file, no. 1203, at the Duval County Courthouse, Probate Court, is not complete. For a complete copy, see Records of the Superior Court, Box 131, File 17, SAHSRL.

Chapter 1. Senegal

1. Mbaye Guèye, paper (untitled) presented at the Anna Kingsley in Senegal Historical Conference, March 11, 2000, Gorée Island.

2. Key sources are Barry, *Senegambia and the Atlantic Slave Trade*, and Searing, *West African Slavery and Atlantic Commerce*. Also of significance are Curtin, *Economic Change in Precolonial Africa*; Lovejoy and Baier, "The Desert-Side Economy of the Central Sudan"; and Lovejoy, *Transformations in Slavery*. See also Robinson, "The Islamic Revolution of Futa Toro" and *Chief and Clerics*, for the impact of Fulbe, Arab, and Berber emirates from Trarza. For Wolof culture, I relied on Gamble, *The Wolof of Senegambia*.

3. Webb discusses the exchange of slaves for horses with Saharan-based merchants in *Desert Frontier*, arguing that the numbers of slave captives taken from Wolof villages for sale across the Sahara exceeded the numbers sold to Europeans. Barry, *Senegambia and the Atlantic Slave Trade*, is persuasive on the destructive impact of European trade on West African society. Diop's "Traite négrière et cadres de vie dans le pays wolof" was informative on the destruction and relocation of rural villages in Jolof and transformation of housing styles. See also Barry, *Le royaume du Waalo le Sénégal avant la conquête*.

4. Charles, "A History of the Kingdom of Jolof (Senegal), 1800–1890." See also Searing, *West African Slavery and Atlantic Commerce*, 10–12. Also helpful was Bomba, "History of the Wolof State of Jolof until 1860" and "The Pre–Nineteenth Century Political Tradition of the Wolof."

5. On the grain trade, see Searing, *West African Slavery and Atlantic Commerce*. For related events in Trarza and Brakna, and for Portuguese

involvement, see Barry, *Senegambia and the Atlantic Slave Trade*, and Robinson, "The Islamic Revolution of Futa Toro."

6. For Kajoor, see Diouf, *Le Kajoor au XIXe siècle.*

7. Barry, *Senegambia and the Atlantic Slave Trade*, 44. Barry sees the kingdom of Kajoor from 1677 as "a perfect example of *ceddo* power" and of the "ubiquitous violence" spread throughout the region. See Webb, *Desert Frontier*, 70–72, 76–81, and 88–96, for horses and cavalry states in the Senegambia. Exchange prices were generally fifteen to thirty captured slaves for every horse. In the early years of trade in Senegambia, Portuguese traders sold horses. For the tyeddo, see Diouf, *Le Kajoor au XIXe siècle*, and Searing, *West African Slavery and Atlantic Commerce.*

8. Maxwell, "Answer to the Questions Proposed by His Majesty's Commissioner for Investigation of the Forts and Settlements in Africa," January 1, 1811.

9. Diop, "Traite négrière," 1, 4.

10. Searing, *West African Slavery and Atlantic Commerce*, 155–62.

11. The conclusion that raids continued into Jolof comes from Diouf, *Le Kajoor au XIXe siècle.* I thank Dr. Diouf for sharing his findings with me in an interview in November 1994 in Dakar, Senegal. Searing, *West African Slavery*, and Barry, *Senegambia and the Atlantic Slave Trade*, explore the religious wars.

12. Commentary on temperature and climate is based on my observations during a journey in March 2000 from Dakar to Jolof and on two previous visits during summer and fall seasons. More important, however, is the careful research in Webb, *Desert Frontier*, chapter 1.

13. Searing, Barry, and others have described the tyeddo and their widespread violence and terror. See also M. Klein, "Servitude among the Wolof and Sereer of Senegambia."

14. For a naturalist's observations, see Adanson, "A Voyage to Senegal, the Isle of Gorée, and the River Gambia." Webb, *Desert Frontier*, 7–14, examines the impact of drought, charcoal production, and herding on forestation in the Senegal Valley.

15. Slaves of the Wolof were generally Sereer or Bambara or from other nations to the east of Senegal. The tyeddo claimed dozens of healthy captives for wives and agricultural laborers. For gender ratios, see H. Klein, "African Women in the Atlantic Slave Trade"; Thornton, "Sexual Demography: The Impact of the Slave Trade on Family Structure"; and M. Klein, "Women in Slavery in the Western Sudan." See also M. Klein, "The Impact of the Atlantic Slave Trade on the Societies of the Western Sudan." M. Klein and Searing see slaving as a monopoly enterprise of kings. European involvement brought sharp increases in the numbers of slave exports, yet more of the slave captives were absorbed in Africa than were exported. The mention of ratios of women is related to discussion in

chapter 2 of a ship that arrived in Cuba in summer 1806 with a high concentration of female slaves aboard.

16. Lloyd to Secretary of State, August 16, 1805, CO 268/7, PRO.

17. Ibid., May 23, 1806. The volume and cost estimates were prepared by a Mr. W. Forbes, then at Sierra Leone.

18. For Kajoor raiding and the Damel's commercial role, see Diouf, *Le Kajoor au XIXe siècle.*

19. See *Gorée: The Island and the Historical Museum.* Little has been published on British-occupied Gorée (1800–1817).

20. See Searing, *West African Slavery and Atlantic Commerce*, 93–128, concerning merchants and slaves at St.-Louis and Gorée.

21. The physical description of Gorée Island is based on my personal observations during visits in 1970, 1994, and 2000.

22. Dr. Christian B. Wadstrom, a Swede who traveled widely in coastal West Africa in the 1780s to collect scientific data, heard from a "signare" that 1,200 slaves could be held in the pens. See C. B. Wadstrom, *Observations on the Slave Trade.*

23. Boufflers to Countess Eléonore de Sabran, undated, quoted in *Gorée: The Island and the Historical Museum*, 16.

24. Brooks, "The Signares of Saint-Louis and Gorée," and Searing, *West African Slavery and Atlantic Commerce*, are excellent on the "métis" traders.

25. Searing, *West African Slavery and Atlantic Commerce*, 93–128.

26. It has not been possible to locate Anta's place of origin precisely. I believe it was in Jolof, but James Searing, an expert on the slave trade in Senegal, considers Kajoor more likely and any of the Wolof states a possibility. The Senegalese historians Mbaye Guèye, Penda Mbow, and Mamadou Diouf suggested Jolof. I thank them and Boubacar Barry for guiding me through the complex history of Senegal in November 1994. Evidence for Anta's age and date of arrival in Florida is given in chapter 3.

27. Monteil, "Le Dyolof et Al-Bouri Ndiaye."

28. This information on Anta's father comes from interviews of Abdou Cissé by Peri Francis, a descendant of Anna Kingsley. Francis lives in Atlanta, Georgia. My conversations with her took place in July and October 1999 at my home in Jacksonville, Florida.

29. My meeting with Abdou Cissé, the griot, in March 2000 produced little of consequence. Ababacar Sy, professor of English at the regional school at Dahra, continued the interviews and wrote to me from Dahra, Senegal.

30. Ababacar Sy, letter of May 19, 2000.

31. Mr. Sy and Abdou Cissé, the griot from Dahra, accompanied me to Yang Yang.

32. Ababacar Sy to the author, May 19, 2000. I surmise that Anta's brothers may have been the eighteenth and twenty-second buurbas rather than the eleventh and twelfth as Mr. Sy concluded. The eleventh and twelfth

buurbas held power during the 1750s rather than the 1850s. See Leyti, "Le Doloff et ses Burbas," and Monteil, "Le Dyolof et Al-Bouri Ndiaye."

33. Dr. Diouf's suggestion came during a conversation in November 1994 in Dakar. He saw parallels between the lives of the *signares* of Gorée and the life of Anna Kingsley in Florida.

Chapter 2. Havana

1. For Havana see Thomas, *Cuba: The Pursuit of Freedom*; Murray, *Odious Commerce*; Kiple, *Blacks in Colonial Cuba, 1774–1899*; Kuethe, "Havana in the Eighteenth Century"; and Lewis, "Anglo Merchants in Cuba in the Eighteenth Century." For slavery in Cuba, see Knight, *Slave Society in Cuba during the Nineteenth Century,* and Paquette, *Sugar Is Made with Blood.*

2. H. Klein, comp., "Slave Trade to Havana, Cuba, 1790–1820." For Danish trade, see Green-Pedersen, "The Scope and Structure of the Danish Negro Slave Trade" and "Colonial Trade under the Danish Flag."

3. H. Klein, "Slave Trade to Havana, Cuba."

4. Eltis et al., "The Trans-Atlantic Slave Trade," a data set compiled under sponsorship of the W.E.B. Du Bois Institute of Harvard University and published in 1999 as a CD-ROM package by Cambridge University Press. Eltis and Richardson suggest the total number who died during the slaving raids and wars in Africa and during the Middle Passage exceeded the number of captives who survived the passage; see "The 'Numbers Game' and Routes to Slavery," along with H. Klein and Engerman, "Long-Term Trends in African Mortality in the Transatlantic Slave Trade." The classic study is Curtin, *The Atlantic Slave Trade: A Census.* Also important are Lovejoy's "The Volume of the Atlantic Slave Trade: A Synthesis" and "The Impact of the Atlantic Slave Trade on Africa: A Review of the Literature," along with David Richardson, "The Eighteenth-Century British Slave Trade," and David Eltis, *Economic Growth and the Ending of the Transatlantic Slave Trade.*

   For contemporary accounts of the Middle Passage, see Falconbridge, *An Account of the Slave Trade,* and Wadstrom, *Observations on the Slave Trade.* H. Klein, *The Atlantic Slave Trade* and *The Middle Passage,* are also valuable, as are Thomas, *The Slave Trade,* esp. 409–30; Anstey and Hair, *Liverpool, the African Slave Trade, and Abolition,* and Rawley, *The Transatlantic Slave Trade.*

5. See Kiple and Higgins, "Mortality Caused by Dehydration during the Middle Passage," and Thomas, *The Slave Trade,* 421–22.

6. Lewis, "Anglo Merchants in Cuba in the Eighteenth Century."

7. Spanish records for 1784–1821, the East Florida Papers (EFP), were invaluable for this study. For Kingsley at Havana in 1806, see EFP R97 B231J18 and EFP R172 B231N21; return to Florida appears in EFP R163

B350U4. See also H. Klein, "Computerized Data on Slave Ships Arriving at Havana, 1790–1821."

8. The Charleston *Courier,* June–September 1806, published numerous references to the *Gustavia* and the *Esther.* I thank Lois Walker, reference librarian at the Dacus Library, Winthrop University, Rock Hill, S.C., for bringing information concerning the sale of the *Gustavia* to my attention. Stephen Behrendt sent information from *Lloyd's List* on arrival of the *Gustavia* in Liverpool. Kingsley's life, including his slave-trading activities and the voyages of 1804–6, is the subject of a biography I am writing. After departing Charleston in 1806, Kingsley traveled first to Natchez, then to Havana. Confirmation for the stops at Cape Town and Mozambique are in Kingsley's letters to and from George Gibbs, his brother-in-law, and to James Hamilton, Charleston merchant. These letters are in in the James Hamilton Papers, Perkins Library, Duke University.

9. See deed of emancipation, EFP R172 B376.

10. For neighbors' testimony, see Patriot War Claims (hereafter PWC), 1812–46, SAHSRL Manuscript Collection 31, File 58, Claim of Anna Madgigine alias Kingsley.

11. EFP R163 B350U4.

12. Mills, *Letters from New-York,* 98.

13. Kingsley's will, probate file 1203, Duval County Courthouse. Legends are in Corse, *Key to the Golden Islands,* and Benjamin, "The Sea Islands."

14. I heard the tale from a tour guide at Kingsley Plantation when it was a Florida state park.

15. EFP R172 B376.

16. The essay on Kingsley originally appeared as Letter XXIII (July 7, 1842) in the *National Anti-Slavery Standard,* the journal published by the abolition organization headed by William Lloyd Garrison. Between August 19, 1841, and May 4, 1843, Child edited the journal and wrote essays titled "Letters from New-York," later collected for a book. Mills, *Letters from New-York,* suggests that only insignificant changes occurred in the transition from journal essay to book, but it is clear from a paragraph in "Letter 33 (August 18, 1842)" quoting Kingsley that Child once possessed detailed interview notes. See 96–102, 190–95, 232–33, and 262.

17. Mills, *Letters from New-York,* 98.

18. Mbow, "Anta Madjiguène Ndiaye, ou le génie de la femme sénégalaise transplanté en Amérique." I thank James Searing for personal correspondence (August 30, 1994) concerning Wolof names. She was Anta, her given name; Majigeen, her mother's given name; and Ndiaye, her father's family name. Villagers would have called her Anta Ndiaye, the child of Majigeen, a sensible way to identify the child and both parents in a polygamous marriage.

Chapter 3. Laurel Grove

1. EFP R125 B289 02 doc. 1810–4 (June 19, 1810, no. 9). For a more detailed treatment, see my "Zephaniah Kingsley's Laurel Grove Plantation, 1803–1813."

2. EFP R62 B144 F12. See also Claim of Zephaniah Kingsley, Superior and Circuit Court Records, Box 131, Folder 16, SAHSRL, and Patriot War Claims, SAHSRL (hereafter ZK [Zephaniah Kingsley] Claim, Superior Court).

3. For identification of East African names, I am obliged to Svend E. Holsoe, personal correspondence, January 10, 1996. Kingsley listed the ethnic identities for several slaves lost in the 1812–13 rebellion: three were Ibo, one Rio Pongo, two "Soo Soo" (Susu today), two New Calabar, three "Zinguibara," and three Calabari. See ZK Claim, Superior Court.

4. EFP R125 B289 02, doc. 1810–4. See also ZK Claim, Superior Court.

5. Deed Book H, March 17, 1828, St. Johns County, says, "Sophy Chidgegane is a woman of Jalof, thirty-six years of age, about five feet high, black complexion." The emancipation entry for Flora Hannahan Kingsley on March 20, 1828, later one of Kingsley's wives, describes her as "a mulatto-colored woman of 20 years of age, a native of Florida and daughter to Sophy Chidgigaine . . . five feet high." Calling Anta and Sophy shipmates is conjecture, but the specific mention of Jolof and the familial relationships that continued at least until 1846, when Abraham witnessed George Kingsley's last will and testament at Puerto Plata, Dominican Republic, is compelling. See Duval County Courthouse, George Kingsley Probate File, no. 1205.

6. PWC, MC 31, File 52, SAHSRL; Schafer, "'A Class of People neither Freemen nor Slaves.'"

7. For Fraser, see my "Family Ties That Bind" and Mouser, "Trade, Coasters, and Conflict in the Rio Pongo from 1790 to 1808" and "Women Slavers of Guinea-Conakry."

8. Will of Francis Richard, Jr., August 10, 1837, Probate File 1756, Duval County. See the *Florida News* (Jacksonville), December 19, 1845, and March 5, 1847, and my "Freedom Was as Close as the St. Johns River." Richard's free black mistress, Teresa, their children Lewis, Michael, and Christiana, Josephine, another mistress (all named in his will), migrated to Puerto Plata, Dominican Republic. See Ortiz, *Emigración de libertos norteamericanos a Puerto Plata en la primera mitad del siglo XIX*, esp. 32.

9. Kingsley, *Treatise*, 7.

10. Ibid., 1.

11. Kingsley, "Address to the Territorial Legislature," 4.

12. EFP R172 B376.

13. ZK Claim, Superior Court.

14. Kingsley's will, Probate File 1203, Duval County Courthouse.

15. EFP R172 B376.

16. EFP R62 B144 F12; ZK Claim and Abraham Hannahan Claim, Box 124, Folder 24, Superior Court.

Chapter 4. The Patriot War

1. Home site information is located in PWC, Box 20, File K-9, Claim of Anna Kingsley, Record Group 599, Spanish Archives, Series 990, Confirmed Claims. Moses Bowden is Box 5, File 51; Uriah Bowden is Box 5, File B-53. William Bardin married Mary Bowden, the widow of Moses. The Creighton property bounded south on Julington Creek. All tracts were on the St. Johns River, between today's County Dock Road and Julington Creek. Horse Landing was owned by the government or Faulk. For Julianton Plantation, see claim of Francis Levett, Treasury 77, Papers of the East Florida Claims Commission, PRO.

2. Some have suggested Anna moved away from Laurel Grove because Zephaniah cohabited with other women. This seems doubtful, given Anna's familiarity with polygamous families in Jolof. This same five-acre site had previously been petitioned for by Enrique Wright, Kingsley's ship captain, to conduct retail trade.

3. PWC 1812–46, SAHSRL, MC 31, File 58, Claim of Anna Madgigine alias Kingsley.

4. Anna Kingsley, ibid. Six hundred bushels of corn were stored in the dwelling in 1813.

5. Landers, *Black Society in Spanish Florida*.

6. For Biassou, see Landers, "Rebellion and Royalism in Spanish Florida."

7. Schafer, "'A Class of People neither Freemen nor Slaves.'"

8. Landers, "African American Women and Their Pursuit of Rights in Eighteenth-Century Texts."

9. Patrick, *Florida Fiasco*.

10. *United States, appellants,* v. *Francis P. Ferreira, administrator of Francis Pass, deceased,* is a key source regarding Kingsley's involvement. He says he was forced to sign a pledge of support or lose his estate. That he eventually became a committed supporter of the insurgency can be seen in letters he wrote in 1812. See his letters in the James Hamilton Papers.

11. Reports of Tomás Llorente, EFP R62 B149 F12 (October 25, November 24, 26, 27, December 13, 17).

12. Moreno to Don Tomás Llorente, November 24, 1813, enclosed in Llorente to Señor Don Sebastián Kindelán, November 26, 1813, EFP R62 B149 F12, doc. 1813-243. Unless otherwise noted, the remaining quoted sections in this chapter come from this source.

13. How Anna was able to converse with Sánchez without being seized by

renegades like Samuel Alexander is unclear. Perhaps Sánchez and his troops were not linked to the marauding bands under Alexander that were rustling cattle and abducting African Americans to sell into slavery in Georgia. Sánchez was white but grew up with and developed close family ties with free persons of color who were his half-brothers and sisters. He would have had close ties to Zephaniah Kingsley and known Anna and her children for many years. That he could have participated in a rebellion to substitute American for Spanish rule in Florida is understandable; that he would have participated in slave raiding and banditry with Alexander is difficult to imagine.

14. Llorente to Kindelán, November 26, 1813, doc. 243, and docs. 250, 255–58, 261, 266, and 269.

Chapter 5. Fort George Island

1. Works Progress Administration, *Spanish Land Grants in Florida*, 4:22–25. Kingsley purchased the plantation in 1817 for $7,000. George J. F. Clarke, East Florida surveyor and planter, arranged the sale. See also Patrick, *Florida Fiasco*, 56–57, and Wildes, "The McIntosh Family of Camden and McIntosh Counties, Georgia, and Alachua and Duval Counties, Florida." Before the fighting began, McIntosh moved his family from Fort George Island to Georgia. McIntosh purchased the property in 1804 from John McQueen, also a migrant from Georgia. McQueen acquired it in 1791 and built the large house on the north end of the island that Kingsley restored.

2. Patrick, *Florida Fiasco*, 259–68, 300–302.

3. Damage is documented in "Case of John H. McIntosh," Patriot War Claims, U.S. Treasury Department Records, FSA.

4. Information about current buildings at Kingsley Plantation is in Stowell, *Timucuan Ecological and Historic Preserve Historic Resource Study*, 67–78. See also Wood, *Jacksonville's Architectural Heritage*, 309–23. For McQueen, see Hartridge, *The Letters of Don Juan McQueen to His Family*.

5. Fretwell, *Kingsley Beatty Gibbs and His Journal of 1840–1843*. A nearby estate in the 1770s, discussed in my "'Yellow Silk Ferret Tied Round Their Wrists,'" is my model for temporary slave housing.

6. For specific detail on Kingsley Plantation, see Fretwell, *Kingsley Beatty Gibbs*. Since Gibbs learned plantation management at Fort George Island, he would likely have followed Zephaniah's practices. On tasking see Morgan, "Work and Culture," and Berlin and Morgan, *The Slaves' Economy*, especially the introduction.

7. Kingsley will. Mary Sammis testified at pension hearings for U.S. Colored Infantry veterans, formerly slaves of her family, that she checked the workers' health every day, presumably following her mother's practices.

8. Álvarez testimony in PWC, MC 31, File 58, Claim of Anna Madgigine. See testimony of John M. Fontane.

9. Wilson, "Notes Concerning the Old Plantation." Quotes that follow in the next few paragraphs are not cited but come from the same typescript.

10. Gamble, *The Wolof of Senegambia*, 34–36, 41–43.

11. Shaw, *Duval County Florida Marriages, 1823–1867*, book O. The May 5, 1831, marriage took place at Saint Johns Bluff, at the time a property of Zephaniah Kingsley. The ceremony was performed by Justice of the Peace Samuel Kingsley.

12. Wilson, "Notes Concerning the Old Plantation." See also Dodge, "An Island by the Sea," and Benjamin, "The Sea Islands."

13. Hann, *A History of the Timucua Indians and Missions*, and Milanich, *Florida Indians and the Invasion from Europe*.

14. Bartram's journal was appended to Dr. William Storke's promotional tract *A Description of East-Florida*. The island was then owned by Richard Hazard.

15. Broadcast indigo plants have been found by staff at Guana River State Park, the site of a 1770s British indigo plantation, and confirmed at the Smithsonian Museum. See the "Indigo File" at the Visitor Center, Guano State Park, South Ponte Vedra, Florida. James R. Ward's *Old Hickory's Town* has a chapter on the Franciscan mission at San Juan del Puerto. Notes from William Jones's careful investigation of the mission site can be seen at Special Collections, the Carpenter Library, University of North Florida.

16. William F. Hawley interview, Works Progress Administration, and *The Arlingtonian* 8 (May 1, 1842).

17. Gritzner, "Tabby in the Coastal Southeast." I have seen old tabby structures along the coast of Senegal between Dakar and Portudal.

18. Wood, *Jacksonville's Architectural Heritage*, 318. Wood says the "arc-shaped configuration" was also used at the Joachim Bulow Plantation in Volusia County, Florida. John Michael Vlach shares Wood's assessment in "Not Mansions . . . But Good Enough."

19. Description of the gardens comes from Wilson, "Notes Concerning the Old Plantation."

20. Benjamin, "The Sea Islands."

21. Stowell, *Timucuan Ecological and Historic Preserve*, 73.

22. Diop, "Traite négrière et cadres de vie dans le pays wolof."

23. I am indebted for these observations to Dr. Sidi Camara of the Ministry of Education and a group of educators from Dakar, the regional school at Bambey, Senegal. I also wish to thank Dr. Camara for assistance with the Anna Kingsley in Senegal Historical Conference in March 2000, and for initiating correspondence with President Abdou Diouf.

24. For the Gibbs and McNeill families, see Fretwell, *Kingsley Beatty Gibbs*, and two typescripts on file at the Kingsley Plantation office: Terence H. E. Webb, "Zephaniah Kingsley" (1991), and Daniel L. Schafer, "Kingsley and Related Families: A Typescript Census Compilation, 1830–1870" (1995).

25. Cathedral Parish Records (St. Augustine), Black Baptisms (microfilm roll 3, entry 650, January 30, 1829).

26. Ibid., and Gannon, *The Cross in the Sand*, 139–49.

27. Madeleine L'Engle, *The Summer of the Great-Grandmother*, 187. I am grateful to Kathryn Strayer for bringing this book to my attention. For further information about Susan P. Fatio, see Gertrude L'Engle, *A Collection of Letters*.

28. M. L'Engle, *The Summer of the Great-Grandmother*, 187.

29. The emancipation notice was filed as a property transaction and recorded in Deed Book H, 152, St. Johns County.

30. Ibid.

31. M. L'Engle, *The Summer of the Great-Grandmother*, 188.

32. Parker, "Men without God or King."

33. M. L'Engle, *Summer of the Great-Grandmother*, 183.

34. Kingsley, *Treatise*, 10.

35. Kingsley's will.

36. Duval County, Archibald Abstracts of Historical Property Records, Book B, 20. Buena Vista and Drayton Island were deeded to George Kingsley; see Deed Book I–J, St. Johns County, 488 (December 20, 1832). See also *Spanish Land Grants in Florida*, 4:6–37.

37. Deed Book I–J, 389 (December 21. 1832), St. Johns County.

38. Duval County, Archibald Abstracts, Book B, 10, 12 (June 26, July 20, August 15, 1831); *Florida Herald* (St. Augustine), August 9, 1832. It is clear from testimony of John Sammis in *William, James and Osceola Kingsley* v. *John and Adele Broward*, Records of the Superior Court, July 8, 1876, that Kingsley resided off and on with Flora at Goodby's Creek from 1832 until she moved to Haiti in 1842. See also Marriage License and Baptismal Record, Box X, "Records Prior to the Establishment of Diocese of St. Augustine in the Bishopric Records Center," St. Joseph's Parish, Mandarin, Florida, and Cathedral Parish Records, St. Augustine Historical Society. Pablo Juan Brugal provided copies of baptismal records for children born to Flora and Zephaniah in Puerto Plata, Dominican Republic. Copies of Kingsley's acknowledgment of his children by Flora—and also his child, Micanopy, by Sarah Murphy—was sent by Ms. Peggy Fried, a descendant of Kingsley and Sarah Murphy.

39. Mahon's *History of the Second Seminole War, 1835–1842* is the classic source. Porter, "Negroes and the Seminole War," is excellent concerning black warriors. For a settler's account of a red/black conspiracy, see Jane Murray Sheldon, untitled and undated memoir, Jacksonville Beaches Historical Society. See also *Jacksonville Courier*, August 7, September 3, 17, October 8, 1835.

40. Leon Pamphile, "Emigration of Black Americans to Haiti, 1821–1863." Charles Collins, a New York City merchant with ties to Kingsley, was

selected by Boyer as principal agent for recruiting free blacks from North America. James Redpath established a Haitian Emigration Bureau in Boston.

41. Probate file 1203, Duval County Courthouse.

42. No marriage records have been found for Martha and Mary Kingsley.

Chapter 6. Refuge in Haiti and Return to Florida

1. Kingsley, *Rural Code of Haiti*, 15–16. Kingsley's letters recounting travel in Haiti are reprinted in Stowell, *Balancing Evils Judiciously*. For an account of more than 6,000 free black Americans who emigrated to this part of Haiti, see Ortiz, *Emigración de libertos norteamericanos a Puerto Plata en la primera mitad del siglo XIX*.

2. From "Survey and Plan, Register of Lands," Puerto Plata, May 23, 1838, Book 92, 2. Ms. Peggy Fried generously supplied a copy of this document. The acreage and $3,000 purchase price is from a Kingsley letter to the *Christian Statesman*, June 30, 1838.

3. Kingsley to the Rev. R. R. Gurley, June 30, 1838, printed in the July 6, 1838, issue of the *Christian Statesman* (Washington, D.C.). Gurley was editor of the newspaper and a member of the American Colonization Society. The letter is reprinted in Stowell, *Balancing Evils Judiciously*, 102–6.

4. Ibid., Kingsley to Gurley. I speculate that Zephaniah brought at least three wives to Haiti because it seems unlikely that he would have left Munsilna McGundo and her family in Florida.

5. Ibid.

6. "Agricultural Directory, Principal Owners of Fincas," from the 1919 Census of Puerto Plata, courtesy of Ms. Peggy Fried.

7. Mills, *Letters from New-York*, 114.

8. I am indebted to Ms. Peggy Fried for correspondence, September 14, 1998, with evidence of the land-apportionment agreement.

9. See Fretwell, *Kingsley Beatty Gibbs*, for dates of travel. Certificate of Naturalization, Children of Zephaniah Kingsley and Flora Hannahan Kingsley, November 1842, Haitian Archives at Puerto Plata, courtesy of Pablo Juan Brugal. Obituary, Saint Augustine *News*, September 30, 1843.

10. Mills, *Letters from New-York*, 99.

11. A complete version of Kingsley's will is in Records of the Superior Court, Box 131, File 16, SAHSRL.

12. Martha Kingsley Baxter and Mary Kingsley Sammis received generous gifts of real estate and personal property prior to the establishment of the Kingsley colony in Haiti. By 1840 their families were among the wealthiest in northeast Florida.

13. The petitions were dated January 26, 1845, and January 26, 1846, ibid.

14. Duval County court records were destroyed by fire in 1901. The most

complete account of the lawsuit may be found ibid. Zephaniah Kingsley's probate file (no. 1203, Duval County Courthouse) contains extensive documentation concerning administration of his estate. For *Kingsley* v. *Broward* see "James K. Kingsley, William and Osceola Kingsley, plaintiffs in Error, vs. Adel E. Broward, Frank Broward et al., Defendants in Error," in Choate, *A Digest of the Decisions of the Supreme Court of Florida* 19: 722–47, FSA. May, "Zephaniah Kingsley, Nonconformist," has an attorney's assessment of the legal challenges.

The petitioners were Martha McNeill, her son William Gibbs McNeill, daughters Catherine McNeill Palmer and Anna McNeill Whistler (married to George W. Whistler), and the daughters of Zephaniah's sister Isabella Kingsley Gibbs, Isabella Gibbs King (married to Ralph King) and Sophia Gibbs Couper.

15. James Johnson, "History of Zephaniah Kingsley and Family," has partial contents of letters from George Kingsley to John S. Sammis. Once part of Probate File 1205, Duval County Courthouse, the original letters are now missing from the file. The merchant vessel was the *Frank Henry*.

16. Alphonso Lockward, oral interview, October 1995, Jacksonville. Mr. Lockward lives in Santo Domingo. Moya Pons, *The Dominican Republic*, chaps. 7–10.

17. In addition to Records of the Superior Court, Box 131, Folder 16, SAHSRL, the most important source for the McNeill lawsuit is "Answer to Petition of Anna Kingsley; Response of Benjamin A. Putnam and Kingsley B. Gibbs, September 5, 1846," File 2, Papers Concerning the Will of Zephaniah Kingsley, 1844, 1846, in M878-020, FSA. For *Kingsley* v. *Broward* see Choate, *A Digest of the Decisions of the Supreme Court of Florida* 19: 722–47, FSA. See also James Johnson, "History of Zephaniah Kingsley and Family," JML.

18. Bethune's communication is in Judge's Order Book, March 2, 1846, Probate Court, Duval County Courthouse. For an even more complicated challenge to inheritance rights, see my "Family Ties That Bind."

19. Attorney Gregory Yale represented Anna before Judge Crabtree. See Yale to Crabtree, August 24, September 7, 1846. On February 1, 1847, Crabtree ordered K. B. Gibbs and Benjamin Putnam, executors, to begin distributing assets to the heirs.

20. Coffee was also deposed by Judge Crabtree. He was listed in the 1850 census as age fifty-five, a surveyor born in Georgia, living with his son-in-law, age thirty-eight, and daughter, age twenty-two, and his grandchildren: John, five, Joshua, four, and Charles, two. The McNeill family is also listed in the 1864 and 1865 Provost Marshal censuses of Jacksonville, where Elizabeth is listed as mulatto.

21. Probate File 1203, Duval County Courthouse.

22. Woodson, "Free Negro Owners of Slaves in the United States," 42. See

also Woodson, *The Mind of the Negro as Reflected by Letters Written during the Crisis, 1800–1860*. For Berlin, see *Slaves without Masters*, 273; for Franklin, *From Slavery to Freedom*, 173.

23. Koger, *Black Slaveowners*, 80–86.
24. Anna purchased the property from James and Sarah Acker. See Archibald Abstracts, Duval County Courthouse. Previous owners of the farm were John S. Sammis, Francis Richard, Gabriel Perpall, and Robert Bigelow.
25. For Deep Creek, see Deed Book I–J, St. Johns County, December 21, 1832, 389. The slaves were Lindo [Kingsley]; Cato and his wife Dorchas and child; Quala and her two children; and Abdallah [Kingsley] and his wife Bella and their children Jim, Elsey, Ann, and Polly. For the tax default, see the December 12, 1851, Deed Book P, 250.

Chapter 7. A Free Black Community in a Time of Race Hysteria

1. My census tallies differ from the official tallies. Free persons of mixed-race backgrounds were counted as white, black, or mulatto depending, apparently, on the census taker and on the gender and social standing of the head of household being tallied. In 1850 and 1860 the census lists Mary Sammis and her children as white even though she was the daughter of an African-born black woman and a white man. Mary's sister, Martha Baxter, along with the Baxter children, were listed as white in 1850 and mulatto in 1860.

My tally includes nonwhites in the households of John S. Sammis, Alonzo Phillips, Toby Kingsley, Mary A. Williams, Maria Kingsley, Lindo Kingsley, Abdallah (Kingsley), Martha B. Baxter, Joseph Mocs, Anna M. Kingsley, Elizabeth King, Cornelia Taylor, George Hagins, John B. Richard, and Charles J. McNeill. Census takers sometimes omitted persons. Albert Sammis, son of John S. Sammis and Antoinette Paine, a slave owned by Sammis, was not listed in 1860 even though he lived with his father. Albert's mother was not listed even though she had been freed and given land and a home near the Sammis family.

For consistency of comparisons, I included Clay County numbers as part of Duval County for 1860. Clay had been carved from Duval in 1858. There was a single free colored family in Clay County in 1860, with seven members in the household.

2. See *Population of the United States in 1860* and the tables in Berlin, *Slaves without Masters*, 46–47, 136–37. See also Ruth B. Barr and Modeste Hargis, "The Voluntary Exile of Free Negroes of Pensacola," 3–5, and Russell Garvin, "The Free Negro in Florida before the Civil War," 9–17.
3. 1860 Census, St. Johns County. Thompson, comp., *Florida Law, Statutes, etc. . . . A Manual*, 533; Smith, *Slavery and Plantation Growth in Antebellum Florida, 1821–1860*, 119–21; Ellsworth and Ellsworth, *Pensacola: The Deep Water City*, 44–45; Barr and Hargis, "The Voluntary Exile of the Free

Negroes of Pensacola," 3–14. For the 1845 Florida state census, see the Jacksonville *News*, February 27, 1846.

4. Another unique community existed in Calhoun County, where the census taker in 1860 recorded five white and twenty-five black or mixed-race persons living in Marianna. William Stafford, a sixty-five-year-old white man from North Carolina lived with Polly Stafford, his fifty-five-year-old mixed-race wife, born in Alabama, and their sixteen-year-old son, Jim. Jack Howard, a twenty-six-year-old mixed-race man, apparently had three wives, each recorded as "White Wife." Perhaps it was the presence of Lotty Howard, Betty Bunch, and Molly Thompson (ages twenty, twenty-three, and twenty-two) in the household headed by a free black male that prompted the census taker to write at the bottom of the form, "The Free Negroes in this county are mixed blooded almost white and have intermarried with a low class of whites. Have no trade occupation or profession. They live in a settlement or town of their own, their personal property consists of cattle and hogs, they make no produce except corn peas and potatoes and very little of that. They are a lazy indolent and worthless race." Ironically, he listed the six households as possessing real estate valued at $4,550.

5. Many of the themes of this chapter are explored in my "A Class of People neither Freemen nor Slaves." See also Garvin, "The Free Negro in Florida before the Civil War"; Bates, "The Legal Status of the Negro in Florida"; and Jackson, "The Negro and the Law in Florida, 1821–1921."

6. Jacksonville *Courier*, December 24, 1835, January 7, 22, 1836; *Florida News* (Jacksonville), May 7, 1847, July 23, 1853; the Jacksonville *Standard*, May 5, 1859. See also Smith, *Slavery and Plantation Growth*, 51, 107, 110–13, 118–21.

7. *East Florida Herald* (St. Augustine), October 23, 1824.

8. Ibid.

9. *Florida Herald*, March 25, 1829; *James F. Clarke* v. *Francis J. Avice*, Records of the Superior Court, St. Johns County, 1829, Box 129, File 103, SAHSRL. For a similar case see *George W. Clarke* v. *State of Florida*, January 12, 1846, Records of the Circuit Court, St. Johns County, Box 98, File 58, SAHSRL. Martin, *Florida during the Territorial Days*, provides information on Florida courts in the period 1821–45.

10. *East Florida Herald*, June 3, 7, 1823; Morris and Maguire, "Beginnings of Popular Government in Florida"; Martin, *Florida during the Territorial Days*, 25–47; Davis, "The Florida Legislative Council, 1822–1838"; Julie Ann Lisenby, "The Free Negro in Antebellum Florida."

11. For the Sutton case, see Schafer, "A Class of People neither Freemen nor Slaves."

12. For testimony of Sutton's white neighbor, John Moore, see Probate File 1876 (May 16, 1846), Duval County Courthouse.

13. See Schafer, "A Class of People neither free men nor Slaves." For primary documentation see Probate File 99 (Jacob Bryan), Duval County Courthouse, and the Jacksonville *News* for December 10, 1847, June 3, July 29, September 23, 1848. The difficulties began with Jacob Bryan's murder by his daughter Celia. During the trial there were unprovable hints of child abuse, but Celia was found guilty of murder. The jury recommended clemency, prompting Governor William D. Mosely to commute the sentence for three months while he investigated Celia's "great hardship." Some residents petitioned the governor asking for mercy for Celia; others demanded her execution. When Celia was hanged, according to the *News* (September 23, 1848), "She met her fate without the least remorse for the crime she had committed, and, up to the last moment, denounced her mother as the cause of her death."

14. Schafer, "A Class of People neither free men nor Slaves." By order of the sheriff, Susan Bryan was sold at a public auction in February 1852.

15. Hogue, "Heirs of Jacob Bryan vs. Dennis, Mary, and Others," 445–46.

16. See Papy, "Amaziah W. Archer, Appellant, vs. Isaiah D. Hart and John S. Sammis, Appellees," 234–60.

17. Genovese, *Roll, Jordan, Roll*, 27.

18. For examples for Duval County, see Sophia Fleming, Probate File 627 (1848), Lewis Christopher, File 355 (1860), and Mariah Doggett, File 500 (1854); for St. Johns County, Susan Murphy, in Wills and Letters of Administration, no. 1, 297 (1855), John M. Fontane, in Order Book A, 7 (1855), and Clarissa Anderson, in Anderson Papers, manuscript collections, SAHSRL.

19. Berlin, *Slaves without Masters*, 141.

20. Genovese, *Roll, Jordan, Roll*, 401.

21. See the Jacksonville *News*, May 15, 22, 29, June 5, 1852.

22. Ibid., June 5, 1852. Slave mechanics were required to pay an annual license fee of $10.50, male laborers $5.50, and female laborers $3.50. The slave "self hire-out" restriction was repealed in 1859, following lobbying efforts by large slaveholders. See the Jacksonville *Standard*, May 5, 1859.

23. The *Florida Republican*, July 19, 1855. For emancipation of two eighteen-year-old sisters by Alberti in 1847, see Nassau County Deed Records, Book A, 197–98 (April 14, 1847).

24. The Alberti controversy is reported in the *Florida Republican* on June 14, July 19, August 9, 1855.

25. Ibid., June 14, 1855.

26. Ibid., August 9, 1855.

27. Papy, *Florida Reports*, 1853, 185–96. I thank Debbi Landi for bringing this case to my attention.

28. Cathedral Parish Records, microfilm roll 3, Colored Baptisms (November 23, 1848). Land purchase is in Archibald Abstracts, Book G, 16 (January

1847), and 285 (July 5, 1854). Jacksonville University encloses Chesterfield today. Probate File 1203, Duval County Courthouse.

29. Deeds of emancipation in Duval County were destroyed by fire in 1901. Probate records, which survived the conflagration, only rarely include emancipations. Most Kingsley emancipations were in St. Johns County. The individuals mentioned here were free and living in the vicinity of Anna and her daughters in 1850 and 1860. She owned fifteen slaves in 1847; they had been under control of John Sammis while she was in Haiti. See Duval County Tax Records, 1840–1860, FSA. Lindo Kingsley apparently changed his name to Wright after the Civil War.

30. Deed of manumission, October 19, 1844, Probate File 1203, Zephaniah Kingsley, Duval County Courthouse.

31. Probate Files 1203, Zephaniah Kingsley, and 1205, George Kingsley, Duval County Courthouse.

32. Ibid., 1205. Note the slave inventories and estate appraisals and account of the 1848 estate sale of personal property in this file. No mentions of Frank and Bill, carpenter William Kingsley's sons, appear after the 1844 inventory. At the 1848 estate auction, Mike's brother, Augustus, and his father, Jenoma, were sold as a "family" to John Jones for $590.

33. Johnson and Roark, *No Chariot Let Down*, 12.

34. Testimony of Albert Sammis, March 8, 1890, Jacksonville, Florida. Given before R.W.D. Parker, Special Examiner. Pension claim of Albert Sammis, Application 136,412, and Certificate 503,989. Pension Records, Union Army, NA. Other deponents included Mary K. Sammis, Egbert C. Sammis, William Johnson, William Cummings, R. M. Lang, George Napoleon, Isaac Edwards, Martha S. Green, C. M. Cooper, Adam Robinson, Duncan James, John Smith, David Hall, John H. Brown, Richard Woods, and Silas Forman. At the time of the interview, Albert Sammis's mother, Antoinette Paine, still lived close by. Most of the men interviewed were Union Army veterans, and most lived in the Arlington area near the old Sammis plantation.

35. Ibid.

36. Ibid.

37. *St. Johns Mirror* (Jacksonville), May 7, 1861.

38. Wood, *Jacksonville's Architectural Heritage*, 244–47. The Duval County censuses for 1850 and 1860, along with the Duval County tax rolls, document Sammis's real and personal property holdings and his agricultural and industrial production at his plantation and sawmill.

39. Anna Kingsley, Probate File no. 1210, Duval County Courthouse.

40. Martha Baxter household, U.S. Census, 1860, Duval County Free Schedules.

41. Anna McNeill Whistler to James McNeill Whistler (her son), March 23, 1858, Whistler Papers, Special Collections Library, Glasgow University. I

am grateful to Professor Evelyn J. Harden of Simon Fraser University, Vancouver, British Columbia, for sending me the story of Charles McNeill's childhood injury (personal correspondence, April 26, 1995). Dr. Harden verified the birth date.

42. The names come from the Duval County censuses of 1850 and 1860 and the provost marshal censuses of 1864 and 1865, copies at the Genealogy Room, JML. Charles is listed separately in 1864 as age seventeen, a government employee living in Jacksonville rather than "Eastside of the St. Johns River," where his parents and siblings resided.

43. Anna McNeill Whistler to James Whistler, March 23, 1858, Whistler Papers.

44. Information on the death of Martha McNeill courtesy of Everett McNeill Kivette, Burnsville, N.C. (personal correspondence, May and June 1999). Mr. Kivette is researching the McNeill family and the migration of Scots Highlanders to North Carolina.

45. Ophelia Moore lived on Pippin Street, Jacksonville, in the 1930s. She was interviewed by James Johnson, Works Progress Administration. See James Johnson, "History of Zephaniah Kingsley and Family."

46. "Sammis Slaves Are Still Alive; Romantic Chapters in Early History Are Recalled," *Florida Times-Union*, June 21, 1925.

47. For the family of Bonify and Mary Napoleon, see Schedule and Appraisement of the Personal Estate and Slaves of Zephaniah Kingsley, Probate File 1203; the sale to Sammis is in File 1205, Probate of George Kingsley, both in the Duval County Courthouse. In the newspaper interview, Esther Lottery said that John Pratt arranged for her family to return to Florida as a reward for securing his family's treasures from marauding Yankee troops.

Chapter 8. Final Flight

1. These general themes are explored in Schafer, "U.S. Territory and State." See also the provocative work by John F. Reiger, "Secession of Florida from the Union—A Minority Decision?"

2. For secession and the war in Florida see Brown, "The Civil War, 1861–1865," and Nulty, *Confederate Florida*.

3. Jacksonville *News*, August 7, 1850.

4. Robinson, "An Account of Some of My Experiences in Florida During the Rise and Progress of the Rebellion," 35.

5. Jacksonville *Standard*, Dec. 6, 1860.

6. Ibid.

7. The "People's Convention" is discussed in Wooster, "The Florida Secession Convention." See also the Jacksonville *Southern Confederacy*, February 1, 1861; Robinson, "An Account of Some of My Experiences"; and Long, *Florida Breezes*, 306–8.

8. Unless otherwise cited, discussion of Civil War Jacksonville is from Martin, *Jacksonville's Ordeal by Fire.*

9. Southern Claims Commission, testimony of John L. Driggs, August 24, 1872, claim no. 16,153 (claim of John S. Sammis). See also claim no. 21,901 (also Sammis) and no. 15,718 (claim of Thomas S. Ells).

10. Testimony of Sammis in claim no. 16,153.

11. Johnson and Roark, *No Chariot Let Down,* 7. See also Johnson and Roark's *Black Masters.* Larry Koger explores these same themes admirably in *Black Slaveowners.*

12. For the blockade see George E. Buker, "St. Augustine and the Union Blockade," *Jacksonville: Riverport-Seaport,* and *Blockaders, Refugees, and Contrabands.*

13. The *New York Times,* March 23, 1862, covers the destruction. See Martin, *Jacksonville's Ordeal by Fire,* chapter 3.

14. See Sherman to the Adjutant General, March 25, 1862, *Official Records of the Army* 1:6; 250.

15. *Florida Union* (Jacksonville), December 31, 1864.

16. Pension claim of Albert Sammis, application 136,412; certificate 503,989. George was living in Jacksonville at the time of the interview, working as a plumber. John L. Driggs said he headed for Fernandina when federal forces arrived there in February 1862, then continued north to New York City, where Sammis joined him in April. He "stayed with him [Sammis] most of the time until the end of the war." See testimony John S. Sammis, claim no. 16,153, Southern Claims Commission.

17. Pension of George K. Sammis, Co. B, 3d New York Infantry; Seventh Battery NYLA, application 677,402; certificate 467,074, Southern Claims Commission. In the Sammis case before the Southern Claims Commission (see note 16), Thomas S. Ells testified that three of Sammis's sons served in Union forces. I have not found the third. Why George enlisted at Newburgh and why he was living in 1919 directly across the Hudson River from Newburgh at Fishkill Landing are puzzling questions. Could one of these have been the wartime residence of his mother, Mary Sammis, and his grandmother, Anna Kingsley?

18. Pension claim of Albert Sammis, Application 136,412, and Certificate 503,989, Pension Records, Union Army, NA.

19. The headstone is in the African-American section of the cemetery. It reads "Theresa Acker, born March 18, 1845, Died April 1, 1863. Erected by her friend, Mary K. Sammis." James and Sarah Acker lived close to the Sammis plantation in the 1840s and after the war. I thank Harold J. Belcher for bringing this monument to my attention. The Army Continental Commands Lists of Persons granted Passes to North by Steamer, Record Group 393, part 1, no. 4286, books 214–15, NA, records passes for Sammis to Philadelphia, July 29, 1864; to Charleston, March 15, 1865; and to New

York, March 21, November 6, 1865. I am grateful to Barbara Tucker for the Army Continental Commands documentation.

20. See Martin, *Jacksonville's Ordeal by Fire*, chaps. 6–8, and Nulty, *Confederate Florida.*

21. *New York Times*, June 3, 1864; *New York Herald*, June 4, 1864; Calvin Robinson, "Manuscript of His Residence in Jacksonville during the Civil War," Box 51, PKY.

22. Copies of the Union Census of Northeast Florida, 1864 and 1865, are at JML; original is S 1489, Department of the South, Census of the District of Florida, Charles E. Coolidge, Seventh U.S. Infantry, Provost Marshal.

23. Other possibilities are New York City, Newburgh, N.Y., Philadelphia, and Washington, D.C.

24. *Florida Union*, Oct. 21, 28, 1865. Copies courtesy of Barbara Tucker. See Newspaper Collections, microfilm roll 3177, Library of Congress, Washington, D.C., and also the Southern Claims Commission, no. 16,153.

Chapter 9. Final Years

1. Based on a study of newspapers and samples of commodity prices in more than a hundred northeast Florida estate inventories from the 1780s to 1860, excluding slave and land values, I estimate that one dollar in 1860 was worth approximately the equivalent of $30 today. See "Composite Commodity Price Index" in Derks, *The Value of a Dollar.*

2. *Population Schedules of the Eighth Census of the United States, 1860.* See William F. Hawley, interview, June 24, 1940, by Rose Shepherd, in "Life History, Works Progress Administration." Hawley saw documents confirming Confederate confiscation of Sammis property in courthouse documents before they were destroyed by the great fire of 1901. See Archibald Abstracts, entries for March 6, 27, 1873.

3. Archibald Abstracts, February 5, 1866. The "Hanson Town" land was purchased from Hilliard and Elizabeth Jones on December 12, 1865. See also Pension Claim of Daniel D. Hanson, Thirty-fourth USC Infantry, application 362,152; certificate 265,104, submitted by Cornelia B. Hanson, widow.

4. Archibald Abstracts, March 6, 1871. See William Hawley, WPA interview, for more on the sawmill.

5. Archibald Abstracts; dates vary from 1866 to 1873. Property is sometimes deeded by John and Mary Sammis to a relative, only to be returned a few years later. To verify the listings one must trace the deed entries line by line in a sometimes disorganized compilation put together by title companies after the great fire of 1901. It is not clear if James Gallison Sammis was a son of Mary and John or a grandson.

6. Archibald Abstracts. For Phillips, see the 1860 Census of Duval County and his Union Army pension record.

7. Anna Whistler to Mr. Gamble, August 3, 1867, from Homeland, Whistler Collection, Glasgow University. A genealogy of Charles McNeill's family prepared by Josephine Flewellen Caldwell, deceased, of Jacksonville, Florida, states that Donald C. McNeill, the eldest son of Charles and Elizabeth Coffee, "lived as a young boy with Mrs. Whistler in Philadelphia" and that the second child born in the family died. Josephine and her husband, Alvan Van Buskirk Caldwell, also deceased, were both descended from Charles Donald (she does not use the commonly cited J. as a middle initial) McNeill and Elizabeth Coffee McNeill. I am grateful to Everett McNeill Kivette for sending me a copy of the genealogy.

8. Whistler to Gamble, September 16, 1867, Whistler Collection.

9. Ibid.

10. Ibid., May 6, 1869.

11. McNeill's will is in Order Books in Probate, Book A, Duval County Courthouse. See microfilm roll 14, 190, JML.

12. From the McNeill genealogy prepared by Josephine F. Caldwell.

13. See, for example, the *Florida Times,* February 8, 1866, and the *New South* (Jacksonville), August 12, 1874.

14. *Population Schedules of the Ninth Census of the United States. 1870. Florida.* See the *Jacksonville City Directory* for 1870, 1882, and 1889.

15. Lena Mooney is identified as the wife of George K. Sammis in his military pension claim. George lived only briefly in Jacksonville after the war, but he resided for several years in the Dominican Republic, the Bahamas, Indian River, Florida, New York City, and Fishkill Landing, N.Y.

16. Martha may also have resided temporarily with her friend Mary A. Richard. Mary resided briefly with Martha in 1850 (see the census entry for Martha Baxter), and the Richard home still stands in the Oak Haven section of Jacksonville. See Wood, *Jacksonville's Architectural Heritage.*

17. Probate file 143, Duval County Probate Records, Martha K. Baxter.

18. Ibid.

19. Probate file 1210, Anna Kingsley, Duval County.

20. Living in the Sammis household in 1870 were John and Mary, Edward G. and Elizabeth and their daughter, Mary M., and Edward C. Koppell, George Jackson, Diana Kingsley, and George D. Sammis. The Archibald Abstracts document that John Sammis owned two properties in Mandarin. Evidence for the 1877 purchase of a gravesite from the Florida Winter Home Association is also in the Archibald Abstracts.

   A legal dispute arose between John Sammis and William Mathews, agent for the Florida Winter Home Association, concerning purchase of the hundred-acre homesite. Among other allegations, Sammis charged that Mathews promised to set aside one-quarter of an acre of land for a Sammis family burial ground but instead executed a deed for a piece of land only twenty feet square. In 1883 the Florida Supreme Court ruled against Sammis. See "John S. Sammis, Appellant, v. William Mathews, Appellee," in Choate, *A Digest of the Decisions of the Supreme Court of Florida* 19: 811–16.

21. The papers are in the possession of Phil May, Jr., of Jacksonville.
22. May's research notes are mostly undated. This one is marked "notes taken during visit to Arlington Cemetery on a Sat. P.m. in April 1940 with prof Wilson & his uncle." The note also states that a Mr. Lilly and a Mr. Bradshaw assisted with the grave marking.

A Personal Postscript

1. Clark, "Landscape of the Rollins Homestead and Cemetery Study."
2. Papers were read by Professor Mbaye Guèye and his colleagues Penda Mbow and Brahim Diop along with Jane Landers of Vanderbilt University, Therese O'Connell of Jacksonville University, Kathryn Tilford of the National Park Service, and me. Messrs. Andre Sanko, then minister of education of Senegal, and Sidi Camara were key supporters in Senegal.

Bibliography

Primary Documents and Document Collections

Cathedral Parish Records. Diocese of St. Augustine Catholic Center, Jacksonville, Florida. Black Baptisms, vols. 1–3. Microfilm at SAHSRL.

East Florida Papers Manuscript Collection. Library of Congress. Microfilm at PKY.

Eltis, David, Stephen D. Behrendt, David Richardson, and Herbert S. Klein. *The Trans-Atlantic Slave Trade: A Database on CD-Rom.* Cambridge: Cambridge University Press, 1999.

Federal Writers' Collection. Federal Works Agency, Work Projects Administration. PKY.

Hamilton, James. Papers, uncataloged. Perkins Library, Duke University.

Hawley, William F. Interview, June 24, 1940, by Rose Shepherd. In "Life History, Works Projects Administration" (typescript files of interviews). JML.

Kingsley, Zephaniah. "Address to the Legislative Council of Florida on the Subject of its Colored Population, by Z. Kingsley, A Planter of That Territory" (c. 1823). State Library of Florida, FSA.

Marriage License and Baptismal Record. "Records Prior to the Establishment of the Diocese of St. Augustine in the Bishopric Records Center." St. Joseph's Parish, Jacksonville, Florida.

McNeill family papers and genealogy. In Dena E. Snodgrass Collection, PKY.

Papers Concerning the Will of Zephaniah Kingsley, 1844, 1846. Record Group 900,000. Series/Collection no. M87–20. FSA.

Patriot War Claims. Spanish Archives, Series 990, Confirmed Claims, Record Group 599. FSA.

Patriot War Papers and Patriot War Claims, 1812–1846. Records of the Circuit and Superior Court. Florida: Northern District. SAHSRL.

Robinson, Calvin. "An Account of Some of My Experiences in Florida During the Rise and Progress of the Rebellion." JHSL. Typescript, undated.

———. "Ms. of Robinson concerning his residence in Jacksonville during the Civil War." MS Box 51. PKY.

United States. District Court (Florida: Northern District). *United States, ap-*

pellants, vs. Francis P. Ferreira, administrator of Francis Pass, deceased. In *Index to the Miscellaneous documents of the Senate of the United States for the First Session of the Thirty-sixth Congress.* Washington, D.C.: George W. Bowmen Printer, 1860.

Whistler, James McNeill. Papers. Special Collections Library, Glasgow University (Scotland).

Wilson, Gertrude Rollins. "Memoir of Mrs. Millar Wilson." Typescript, Spring 1952. JHSL.

————. "Notes Concerning the Old Plantation, Fort George Island." Undated typescript, JHSL.

Works Progress Administration. The Slave Narrative Collection, Typescript files, JML.

Public Records

"An act for the relief of the heirs of Jacob Bryan." *Journal of the State of Florida, at its Fifth Session* (Tallahassee, 1851), 71, 100, 109, 133, 157.

Agriculture of the United States in 1860, Compiled from the Original Returns of the Eighth Census. Washington, D.C.: Government Printing Office, 1864.

Carter, Clarence E., comp. *Territorial Papers of the United States.* Vols. 22–26, *Florida Territory.* Washington, D.C.: Gales and Seaton, 1822.

Choate, Charles A., comp. *A Digest of the Decisions of the Supreme Court of Florida, Volumes I to XXIV inclusive.* St. Louis, Mo.: F. H. Thomas Law Book Co., 1889. FSA.

Clay County Courthouse, Green Cove Springs, Florida. Deed records.

————. Tax records, 1859–1880. Microfilm copies (roll JR 3865–3866), FSA.

Compendium of the Seventh Census, 1850, Agriculture. Washington, D.C.: Government Printing Office, 1854.

Duval County Courthouse, Jacksonville, Florida. "Archibald Abstracts of Historical Property Records, 1821–1901." Probate Court, Annex.

————. Judge's Order Book, February 20, March 2, 1846. Probate Court.

————. Marriage Records. Clerk of Court's Office.

————. Order Books in Probate. Book A: 1845–1866. Book B: 1866–1878. Probate Court. Microfilm roll 14, JML.

————. Probate records. Probate Court.

————. Tax Records, 1846–1860, 1866–1869, 1872–1875, 1876–1877. Microfilm copies (rolls JR 3869–3871), FSA.

Fifth Census or Enumeration of the Inhabitants of the United States as Corrected at the Department of State, 1830. Washington, D.C.: Duff Green, 1832.

Florida State Archives. Tallahassee, Florida. Record Group 900,000, Series/Collection no. M87-020, Papers Concerning the Will of Zephaniah Kingsley, 1844, 1846.

Great Britain. PRO. CO, Series 267, file 29. Original Correspondence of the Secretary of State. Series 267, vol. 29, January 1, 1811. Answers to the

Questions Proposed to Lt. Colonel Maxwell, Lieutenant Governor of Senegal and Gorée by His Majesty's Commissioner for Investigating the Forts and Settlements in Africa.

————. Series 268, files 7 and 23. Letters to the Secretary of State: Despatches from Gorée.

————. Treasury 77. Papers of the East Florida Claims Commission.

Hogue, David P., reporter. "Heirs of Jacob Bryan vs. Dennis, Mary, and Others." *Florida Reports: Reports of Cases Argued and Adjudged in the Supreme Court of Florida* 4 (1852). Tallahassee: Joseph Clisby, *Florida Sentinel*, 1849–76. FSA.

Jacksonville, Florida. *Ordinances of the Town of Jacksonville of 1859.* Jacksonville: Columbus Drew, 1859.

Journals of the Proceedings of the Senate of the General Assembly of the State of Florida. Sixth Session. Tallahassee: Joseph Clisby, *Florida Sentinel*, Printer to the Senate. 1853. FSA.

Kingsley, Zephaniah. Will [incomplete copy], Probate Court, file, no. 1203. Duval County Courthouse, Jacksonville, Florida.

————. Will [complete copy]. Martha McNeill et al. vs. Kingsley B. Gibbs and Benjamin A. Putnam. Records of the Superior Court, Box 131, File 17. SAHSRL.

Memorial Petition to the Superior Court for the District of North Florida, Claim of Zephaniah Kingsley, 1812–13. PKY.

Nassau County Courthouse, Fernandina, Florida. Deed books.

————. Tax records, 1845–1869. Microfilm copy (roll JR 3865), FSA.

National Archives. Record Group 15. Records of the Veterans Administration. Pension Records. Union Army, United States Colored Infantry.

————. Record Group 56. Department of the Treasury. Records of the Southern Claims Commission.

————. Record Group 94. Compiled Service Records of Volunteer Soldiers Who Served with United States Colored Troops. Regimental Muster and Descriptive Books. United States Colored Infantry.

————. Record Group 393. Department of the South. "Lists of Persons Granted Passes to go North by Steamer."

————. Record Group 393. "Union Army Census of Northeast Florida, 1864 and 1865." Department of the South, Census of the District of Florida, Charles E. Coolidge, Seventh U.S. Infantry, Provost Marshal.

The Official Records of the Union and Confederate Navies in the War of the Rebellion. 30 vols. Washington, D.C.: Government Printing Office, 1894–1922.

Papy, Mariano D. "Amaziah W. Archer, Appellant, vs. Isaiah D. Hart and John S. Sammis, Appellees." *Florida Reports: Reports of Cases Argued and Adjudged in the Supreme Court of Florida* 6 (1854). Tallahassee: Joseph Clisby, *Florida Sentinel*, 1849–76. FSA.

————. "Luke, a Slave, Plaintiff in Error, vs. The State of Florida." *Florida Reports: Reports of Cases Argued and Adjudged in the Supreme Court of Florida* 5 (1853). Tallahassee: Joseph Clisby, *Florida Sentinel*, 1849–76. FSA.

Population of the United States in 1860; Compiled from the Original Returns of the Eighth Census. Washington, D.C.: Government Printing Office, 1864.

Population Schedules of the Ninth Census of the United States. 1870. Florida. Washington, D.C.: Government Printing Office, 1900.

Records of the Superior and Circuit Courts. Florida: Northern and Eastern District. SAHSRL.

St. Johns County Courthouse, St. Augustine, Florida. Office of the Clerk of Court.

————. Deed books.

————. Marriage records.

————. Tax records, 1829–1835, 1845–1856, 1859–1869. Microfilm copies (rolls JR 3902–3903), FSA.

————. Will and probate records.

Santo Domingo, Dominican Republic. National Archives. "Survey and Plan, Register of Lands, Puerto Plata," May 23, 1838. Book 92, page 2.

————. "Agricultural Directory, Principal Owners of Fincas." Census of 1919, Puerto Plata, Dominican Republic.

Seventh Census of the United States, 1850. Washington, D.C.: Government Printing Office, 1853–55.

Shaw, Aurora C., comp. *Duval County Florida Marriages, 1823–1867.* Book "O," 1823–1846, Book "o–1," 1845–1867. Jacksonville: A. C. Shaw, 1983. JML.

Sixth Census or Enumeration of the Inhabitants of the United States, 1840. Washington, D.C.: Rives and Blair, 1841.

Thompson, Leslie A., comp. *A Manual or Digest of the Statute Law of the State of Florida, 1821–1847.* Boston, C. C. Little and J. Brown, 1847. FSA.

The War of the Rebellion: A Compilation of the Official Records of the Union and Confederate Armies. Washington, D.C.: Government Printing Office, 1880–1901.

Work Projects Administration. The Historical Records Survey, Division of Community Service Programs. *Spanish Land Grants in Florida.* Tallahassee, 1941.

Newspapers

The Arlingtonian, May 1, 1842, Special Collections, Jacksonville University Library, Jacksonville, Florida.

Charleston (S.C.) *Courier,* September 23, 1806.

Christian Statesman (Washington, D.C.), July 6, 1838.

Florida Herald (St. Augustine), August 9, 1832.

The Florida News (Jacksonville), December 19, 1845, March 5, 1847.
The Florida Republican (Jacksonville), June 14, July 19, August 9, 1855.
Florida Union (Jacksonville), December 31, 1864, October 21, 28, 1865. Newspaper Collections, microfilm roll 3177, Library of Congress.
The Jacksonville News, December 10, 1847, June 3, July 29, September 23, 1848, August 7, 1850, May 15, 22, 29, June 5, 1852.
Southern Confederacy (Jacksonville), February 1, 1861.
Times-Union (Jacksonville), June 21, 1925.

Secondary Sources

Adanson, Michael. "A Voyage to Senegal, the Isle of Gorée, and the River Gambia." In *A General Collection of the Best and Most Interesting Voyages and Travels in All Parts of the World*, edited by John Pinkerton. Philadelphia: Kimber and Conrad, 1810–12.

Anstey, Roger, and P.E.H. Hair, eds. *Liverpool, the African Slave Trade, and Abolition: Essays to Illustrate Current Knowledge.* Liverpool: Historic Society of Lancashire and Cheshire, 1976.

Barr, Ruth B., and Modeste Hargis. "The Voluntary Exile of Free Negroes of Pensacola." *Florida Historical Quarterly* 17 (July 1938): 3–14.

Barry, Boubacar. *Le royaume du Waalo le Sénégal avant la conquête.* Paris: Éditions Karthala, 1985.

———. *Senegambia and the Atlantic Slave Trade.* Cambridge: Cambridge University Press, 1998.

Bates, Thelma. "The Legal Status of the Negro in Florida." *Florida Historical Quarterly* 6, no. 3 (1928): 159–81.

Benjamin, Samuel G. W. "The Sea Islands." *Harpers New Monthly Magazine* (November 1878): 839–46.

Berlin, Ira. *Many Thousands Gone: The First Two Centuries of Slavery in North America.* Cambridge, Mass.: Harvard University Press, 1998.

———. *Slaves without Masters: The Free Negro in the Antebellum South.* New York: Pantheon, 1974.

Berlin, Ira, and Philip D. Morgan, eds. *The Slaves' Economy: Independent Production by Slaves in the Americas.* London: Frank Cass, 1991.

Bomba, Victoria. "History of the Wolof State of Jolof until 1860, Including Comparative Data from the Wolof State of Walo." Ph.D. diss., University of Wisconsin, 1969.

Brooks, George E. "The Signares of Saint-Louis and Gorée: Women Entrepreneurs in Eighteenth-Century Senegal." In *Women in Africa: Studies in Social and Economic Change*, edited by Nancy J. Hafkin and Edna G. Bay. Stanford, Calif.: Stanford University Press, 1976.

Brown, Canter, Jr. "The Civil War, 1861–1865." In *The New History of Florida*, edited by Michael Gannon, 231–48. Gainesville: University Press of Florida.

————. "Race Relations in Territorial Florida, 1821–1845." *Florida Historical Quarterly* 73 (January 1995): 287–307.

Buettinger, Craig. "Masters on Trial: The Enforcement of Laws against Self-Hire by Slaves in Jacksonville and Palatka, Florida." *Civil War History* 46 (June 2000): 96–106.

Buker, George E. *Blockaders, Refugees, & Contrabands: Civil War on Florida's Gulf Coast, 1861–1865.* Tuscaloosa: University of Alabama Press, 1993.

————. *Jacksonville: Riverport-Seaport.* Columbia: University of South Carolina Press, 1992.

Charles, Eunice A. "A History of the Kingdom of Jolof (Senegal), 1800–1890." Ph.D. diss., Boston University, 1973.

Clark, Carol D. "Landscape of the Rollins Homestead and Cemetery Study." Typescript, University of North Florida, Department of History, Jacksonville, 1999.

Cohen, David W., and Jack P. Greene, eds. *Neither Slave nor Free: The Freedmen of African Descent in the Slave Societies of the New World.* Baltimore: Johns Hopkins University Press, 1972.

Corse, Carita Doggett. *The Key to the Golden Islands.* Chapel Hill: University of North Carolina Press, 1931.

Curry, Leonard P. *The Free Black in Urban America, 1800–1850: The Shadow of the Dream.* Chicago: University of Chicago Press, 1981.

Curtin, Philip D. *The Atlantic Slave Trade: A Census.* Madison: University of Wisconsin Press, 1969.

————. *Economic Change in Precolonial Africa: Senegal in the Era of the Slave Trade.* Madison: University of Wisconsin Press, 1975.

Davis, Edwin Adams, and William Ransom Hogan. *The Barber of Natchez.* Baton Rouge: Louisiana State University Press, 1954.

Davis, William Graham. "The Florida Legislative Council, 1822–1838." Master's thesis, Florida State University, 1970.

Degler, Carl N. *Neither Black nor White: Slavery and Race Relations in Brazil and the United States.* New York: Macmillan, 1971.

Derks, Scott, ed. *The Value of a Dollar: Prices and Incomes in the United States, 1860–1989.* Detroit: Gale, 1994.

Diop, Brahim. "Traite negrière et cadres de vie dans le pays wolof." Paper presented at the Anna Kingsley in Senegal Historical Conference, Gorée Island, March 2000.

Diouf, Mamadou. *Le Kajoor au XIXe siècle.* Paris: Éditions Karthala, 1990.

Dodge, Julia B. "An Island by the Sea." *Scribner's Magazine* (September 1877).

Ellsworth, Lucius, and Linda Ellsworth. *Pensacola: The Deep Water City.* Tulsa, Oklahoma: Continental Heritage Press, 1982.

Eltis, David. *The Rise of African Slavery in the Americas.* Cambridge: Cambridge University Press, 2000.

————. *Economic Growth and the Ending of the Transatlantic Slave Trade.* New York: Oxford University Press, 1987.

Eltis, David, and David Richardson. "The 'Numbers Game' and Routes to Slavery." *Slavery and Abolition: A Journal of Slave and Post-Slave Studies* 18 (April 1997): 1–15.

Falconbridge, Alexander. *An Account of the Slave Trade.* London: J. Phillips, 1788.

Federal Writers' Project. *Slave Narratives: A Folk History of Slavery in the United States, from Interviews with Former Slaves.* 17 vols. St. Clair Shores, Mich.: Scholarly Press, 1976.

Fields, Barbara Jeanne. *Slavery and Freedom on the Middle Ground: Maryland during the Nineteenth Century.* New Haven: Yale University Press, 1985.

Franklin, John Hope, and Alfred A. Moss Jr. *From Slavery to Freedom: A History of African Americans.* New York: Alfred A. Knopf, 1967.

Fretwell, Jacqueline K., ed. *Kingsley Beatty Gibbs and His Journal of 1840–1843.* St. Augustine, Fla.: St. Augustine Historical Society, 1984.

Gamble, David P. *The Wolof of Senegambia: Together with Notes on the Lebu and the Serer.* London: International African Institute, 1967.

Gannon, Michael V. *The Cross in the Sand: The Early Catholic Church in Florida, 1513–1870.* Gainesville: University Presses of Florida, 1983.

Garvin, Russell. "The Free Negro in Florida Before the Civil War." *Florida Historical Quarterly* 46 (July 1967): 9–17.

Genovese, Eugene D. *Roll, Jordan, Roll: The World the Slaves Made.* New York: Pantheon Books, 1974.

Gorée: The Island and the Historical Museum. Dakar, Senegal: IFAN and the Historical Museum, Cheikh Anta Diop University, 1993.

Green-Pedersen, Svend E. "Colonial Trade under the Danish Flag: A Case Study of the Danish Slave Trade to Cuba, 1790–1807." *Scandinavian Journal of History* 5 (1980): 93–120.

————. "The Scope and Structure of the Danish Negro Slave Trade." *Scandinavian Economic History Review* 19 (1971): 149–97.

Gritzner, Janet. "Tabby in the Coastal Southeast: The Culture History of an American Building Material." Ph.D. diss., Louisiana State University, 1978.

Guèye, Mbaye. Opening Remarks. Untitled paper presented at the Anna Kingsley in Senegal Historical Conference, Gorée Island, March 2000.

Hann, John. *A History of the Timucua Indians and Missions.* Gainesville: University Press of Florida, 1996.

Hartridge, Walter Charlton. *The Letters of Don Juan McQueen to His Family: Written from Spanish East Florida, 1791–1807.* Columbia, S.C.: Bostick and Thornley, 1943.

Hill, Louise Biles. "George J. F. Clarke, 1774–1836." *Florida Historical Quarterly* 21 (January 1943): 197–253.

Hogan, William Ransom, and Edwin Adams Davis, eds. *William Johnson's Natchez: The Antebellum Diary of a Free Negro.* Baton Rouge: Louisiana State University Press, 1951.

Jackson, Jesse J. "The Negro and the Law in Florida, 1821–1921." Master's thesis, Florida State University, 1960.

Jacksonville City Directory and Business Advertiser for 1870. Jacksonville: Florida Union Book and Job Office, 1870.

Johns, John E. *Florida during the Civil War.* Gainesville: University of Florida Press, 1963.

Johnson, James. "History of Zephaniah Kingsley and Family." Typescript, ca. 1940. Work Projects Administration files, JML.

Johnson, Michael P., and James L. Roark. *Black Masters: A Free Family of Color in the Old South.* New York: Norton, 1984.

————. *No Chariot Let Down: Charleston's Free People of Color on the Eve of the Civil War.* Chapel Hill: University of North Carolina Press, 1984.

Joyner, Charles. *Down by the Riverside: A South Carolina Slave Community.* Urbana: University of Illinois Press, 1984.

Kingsley, Zephaniah. *The Rural Code of Haiti; Literally Translated from a Publication by the Government Press; Together with Letters from that Country Concerning its Present Condition, by a Southern Planter.* Middletown, N.J.: George H. Evans, 1837.

————. *A Treatise on the Patriarchal or Cooperative System of Society as It Exists in Some Governments, and Colonies in America, and in the United States under the Name of Slavery with Its Necessity and Advantages.* Freeport, N.Y.: Books for Libraries Press, 1970 (reprint of the 1829 ed.).

Kiple, Kenneth F. *Blacks in Colonial Cuba, 1774–1899.* Gainesville: University of Florida Press, 1976.

Kiple, Kenneth F., and Brian T. Higgins. "Mortality Caused by Dehydration during the Middle Passage." In *The Atlantic Slave Trade: Effects on Economies, Societies, and Peoples in Africa, the Americas, and Europe,* edited by Joseph E. Inikori and Stanley L. Engerman. Durham, N.C.: Duke University Press, 1992.

Klein, Herbert S. "African Women in the Atlantic Slave Trade." In *Women and Slavery in Africa,* edited by Clare C. Robertson and Martin A. Klein. Madison: University of Wisconsin Press, 1983.

————. *The Atlantic Slave Trade.* Cambridge: Cambridge University Press, 1999.

————. *The Middle Passage: Comparative Studies in the Atlantic Slave Trade.* Princeton, N.J.: Princeton University Press, 1978.

————, comp. "Slave Trade to Havana, Cuba, 1790–1820." Computer file. Madison: University of Wisconsin Data and Program Library Service, 1978.

Klein, Herbert S., and Stanley L. Engerman. "Long-Term Trends in African Mortality in the Transatlantic Slave Trade." *Slavery and Abolition: A Journal of Slave and Post-Slave Studies* 18 (April 1997): 36–48.

Klein, Martin A. "Women in Slavery in the Western Sudan." In *Women and Slavery in Africa*, edited by Clare C. Robertson and Martin A. Klein. Madison: University of Wisconsin Press, 1983.

———. "The Impact of the Atlantic Slave Trade on the Societies of the Western Sudan." In *The Atlantic Slave Trade: Effects on Economies, Societies, and Peoples in Africa, the Americas, and Europe*, edited by Joseph E. Inikori and Stanley L. Engerman. Durham, N.C.: Duke University Press, 1992.

———. "Servitude among the Wolof and Sereer of Senegambia." In *Slavery in Africa*, edited by Igor Kopytoff and Suzanne Miers. Madison: University of Wisconsin Press, 1983.

Knight, Franklin. *Slave Society in Cuba during the Nineteenth Century*. Madison: University of Wisconsin Press, 1970.

Koger, Larry. *Black Slaveowners: Free Black Slave Masters in South Carolina, 1790–1860*. Jefferson, N.C.: McFarland, 1985.

Kuethe, Allan J. "Havana in the Eighteenth Century." In *Atlantic Port Cities: Economy, Culture, and Society in the Atlantic World, 1650–1850*, edited by Franklin W. Knight and Peggy K. Liss. Knoxville: University of Tennessee Press, 1991.

Landers, Jane G. "African American Women and Their Pursuit of Rights in Eighteenth-Century Texts." In *Haunted Bodies: Gender and Southern Texts*, edited by Anne Goodwyn Jones and Susan V. Donaldson. Charlottesville: University Press of Virginia, 1998.

———. *Black Society in Spanish Florida*. Urbana: University of Illinois Press, 1999.

———. "Rebellion and Royalism in Spanish Florida: The French Revolution on Spain's Northern Colonial Frontier." In *A Turbulent Time: The French Revolution and the Greater Caribbean*, edited by David Barry Gaspar and David Patrick Geggus, 156–77. Bloomington: Indiana University Press, 1997.

L'Engle, Gertrude. *A Collection of Letters, Information and Data on Our Family*. 2 vols. Jacksonville, Fla.: privately printed, 1949.

L'Engle, Madeleine. *The Summer of the Great-Grandmother*. New York: Farrar, Straus and Giroux, 1974.

Lewis, James. "Anglo Merchants in Cuba in the Eighteenth Century." In *The North American Role in the Spanish Imperial Economy, 1760–1819*, edited by Jacques A. Barbier and Allan J. Kuethe. Dover, N.H: Manchester University Press, 1984.

Leyti, Oumar Ndiaye. "Le Doloff et ses bourbas." *BIFAN*, series B, vol. 31 (1969): 966–1008.

Lisenby, Julie Ann. "The Free Negro in Antebellum Florida." Master's thesis, Florida State University, 1967.

Long, Ellen Call. *Florida Breezes; or, Florida, New and Old.* Jacksonville: Ashmead Bros., 1882. Reprint, Gainesville: University of Florida Press, 1962.

Lovejoy, Paul. "The Impact of the Atlantic Slave Trade on Africa: A Review of the Literature." *Journal of African History* 30 (1989): 365–94.

———. *Transformations in Slavery: A History of Slavery in Africa.* Cambridge: Cambridge University Press, 1983.

———. "The Volume of the Atlantic Slave Trade: A Synthesis." *Journal of African History* 23 (1982): 473–501.

Lovejoy, Paul, and Steven Baier. "The Desert-Side Economy of the Central Sudan." *International Journal of African Historical Studies* 8, no. 4 (1975).

Mahon, John K. *History of the Second Seminole War.* Gainesville: University of Florida Press, 1967.

Martin, Richard A., with Daniel L. Schafer. *Jacksonville's Ordeal by Fire: A Civil War History.* Jacksonville: Florida Publishing Company, 1984.

Martin, Sidney Walter. *Florida during the Territorial Days.* Athens: University of Georgia Press, 1944.

May, Philip S. "Zephaniah Kingsley: Non-Conformist, 1765–1843." *Florida Historical Quarterly* 23 (January 1945): 145–59.

Mbow, Penda. "Anta Madjiguène Ndiaye, ou le génie de la femme sénégalaise transplanté en Amérique." Paper read at the Anna Kingsley in Senegal Historical Conference, Gorée Island, March 2000.

Milanich, Jerald. *Florida Indians and the Invasion from Europe.* Gainesville: University Press of Florida, 1995.

Mills, Bruce, ed. *Letters from New-York: Lydia Maria Child.* Athens: University of Georgia Press, 1998.

Monteil, Vincent. "Le Dyolof et Al-Bouri Ndiaye." *BIFAN* 28, no. 3–4 (1996): 595–620.

Morgan, Philip D. "Work and Culture: The Task System and the World of Low Country Blacks, 1700–1880." *William and Mary Quarterly* 39 (October 1982): 563–99.

Mormino, Gary R., ed. "Florida Slave Narratives." *Florida Historical Quarterly* 66 (April 1988): 399–419.

Morris, Allen, and Amelia Rea Maguire. "Beginnings of Popular Government in Florida." *Florida Historical Quarterly* 46 (July 1967): 9–17.

Mouser, Bruce L. "Trade, Coasters, and Conflict in the Rio Pongo from 1790 to 1808." *Journal of African History* 14 (January 1973): 45–64.

———. "Women Slavers of Guinea-Conakry." In *Women and Slavery in Africa,* edited by Clare C. Robertson and Martin A. Klein. Madison: University of Wisconsin Press, 1983.

Moya Pons, Frank. *The Dominican Republic: A National History.* New Rochelle, N.Y.: Hispaniola Books, 1995.

Murray, David R. *Odious Commerce: Britain, Spain and the Abolition of the Cuban Slave Trade.* Cambridge, Mass.: Harvard University Press, 1980.

Nulty, William F. *Confederate Florida: The Road to Olustee.* Tuscaloosa: University of Alabama Press, 1990.

Ortiz, José Augusto Puig. *Emigración de libertos norteamericanos a Puerto Plata en la primera mitad del siglo XIX.* Puerto Plata, Dominican Republic: La Iglesia Metodista Wesleyana, 1978.

Pamphile, Leon D. "Emigration of Black Americans to Haiti, 1821–1863." *The Crisis* 90 (1983): 43–44.

———. *Haitians and African Americans: A Heritage of Tragedy and Hope.* Gainesville: University Press of Florida, 2001.

Paquette, Robert L. *Sugar Is Made with Blood: The Conspiracy of La Escalera and the Conflict between Empires over Slavery in Cuba.* Middletown, Conn.: Wesleyan University Press, 1988.

Parker, Susan R. "Men without God or King: Rural Settlers of East Florida, 1784–1790." *Florida Historical Quarterly* 69 (1990): 135–55.

Patrick, Rembert W. *Florida Fiasco: Rampant Rebels on the Georgia-Florida Frontier, 1810–1815.* Athens: University of Georgia Press, 1954.

Patterson, Steven. "The Social and Economic Position of a Mixed-Race Family in Post–Civil War Jacksonville, Florida." Typescript, April 30, 1993. Department of History, University of North Florida.

Porter, Kenneth W. "Negroes and the Seminole War." *Journal of Southern History* 30 (1964): 427–50.

Rawley, James A. *The Transatlantic Slave Trade.* New York: Norton, 1981.

Reiger, John F. "Secession of Florida from the Union—A Minority Decision?" *Florida Historical Quarterly* 46 (1968): 358–68.

Richardson, Barbara. "A History of Blacks in Jacksonville, Florida, 1860–1895: A Socio-Economic and Political Study." Ph.D. diss., Carnegie-Mellon University, 1975.

Richardson, David. "The Eighteenth-Century British Slave Trade: Estimates of its Volume and Distribution in Africa." *Research in Economic History* 12 (1988): 151–95.

Rivers, Larry E. *Slavery in Florida: Territorial Days to Emancipation.* Gainesville: University Press of Florida, 2000.

Robinson, David. *Chiefs and Clerics: Abu Bokar Kan and Futa Toro, 1853–1891.* New York: Oxford University Press, 1975.

———. "The Islamic Revolution of Futa Toro." *International Journal of African Historical Studies* 8 (1975): 185–211.

Schafer, Daniel L. " 'A class of People neither Freemen nor Slaves': From Spanish to American Race Relations in Florida, 1821–1861." *Journal of Social History* 26 (1993): 587–609.

———. *Anna Kingsley.* 2d rev. ed. St. Augustine, Fla.: St. Augustine Historical Society, 1997.

————. "Family Ties That Bind: Anglo-African Slave Traders in Africa and Florida, John Fraser and His Descendants." *Slavery and Abolition: A Journal of Slave and Post-Slave Studies* 20 (1999): 1–21.

————. "Freedom Was as Close as the River: African Americans and the Civil War in Northeast Florida." In *The African American Heritage of Florida*, edited by David R. Colburn and Jane L. Landers. Gainesville: University Press of Florida, 1995.

————. "Shades of Freedom: Anna Kingsley in Senegal, Florida and Haiti." In *Against the Odds: Free Blacks in the Slave Societies of the Americas*, edited by Jane G. Landers. London: Frank Cass, 1996.

————. "U.S. Territory and State." In *The New History of Florida*, edited by Michael Gannon. Gainesville: University Press of Florida, 1996.

————. " 'Yellow Silk Ferret Tied Round Their Wrists': African Americans in British East Florida, 1763–1784." In *The African American Heritage of Florida*, edited by David R. Colburn and Jane L. Landers. Gainesville: University Press of Florida, 1995.

————. "Zephaniah Kingsley's Laurel Grove Plantation, 1803–1813." In *Colonial Plantations and Economy in Florida*, edited by Jane G. Landers. Gainesville: University Press of Florida, 2000.

Searing, James. *West African Slavery and Atlantic Commerce: The Senegal River Valley, 1700–1860*. Cambridge: Cambridge University Press, 1993.

Smith, Julia Floyd. *Slavery and Plantation Growth in Antebellum Florida, 1821–1860*. Gainesville: University of Florida Press, 1973.

Storke, William. *A Description of East-Florida, with a Journal Kept by John Bartram of Philadelphia, Botanist to His Majesty for the Floridas*. London, 1769.

Stowell, Daniel W. *Balancing Evils Judiciously: The Proslavery Writings of Zephaniah Kingsley*. Gainesville: University Press of Florida, 2000.

————. *Timucuan Ecological and Historic Preserve Historic Resource Study*. Atlanta: National Park Service Southeast Field Area, 1996.

Thomas, Hugh. *Cuba: The Pursuit of Freedom*. New York: Harper and Row, 1971.

————. *The Slave Trade: The Story of the Atlantic Slave Trade, 1440–1870*. New York: Simon and Schuster, 1997.

Thornton, John. "Sexual Demography: The Impact of the Slave Trade on Family Structure." In *Women and Slavery in Africa*, edited by Clare C. Robertson and Martin A. Klein. Madison: University of Wisconsin Press, 1983.

Vlach, John Michael. "Not Mansions . . . But Good Enough: Slave Quarters as Bi-Cultural Expression." In *Black and White Cultural Interaction in the Antebellum South*, edited by Ted Owenby. Jackson: University Press of Mississippi, 1993.

Wadstrom, Christian B. *Observations on the Slave Trade and a Description of*

Some Part of the Coast of Guinea during a Voyage Made in 1787 and 1788. Vol. 1. London: J. Philips, 1789.

Ward, James R. *Old Hickory's Town: An Illustrated History of Jacksonville.* Jacksonville: Florida Publishing Co., 1982.

Webb, James L. A., Jr. *Desert Frontier: Ecological and Economic Change along the Western Sahel, 1600–1850.* Madison: University of Wisconsin Press, 1995.

Webb's Jacksonville City Directory for 1882, including East Jacksonville, Springfield, Hansontown, LaVilla, Brooklyn, and Riverside. New York: Webb Brothers, 1882.

Webb's Jacksonville Directory. Jacksonville, Florida: Wanton S. Webb, 1889.

Wikramanayake, Marina. *A World in Shadow: The Free Black in Antebellum South Carolina.* Columbia: University of South Carolina Press, 1973.

Wildes, Tara. "The McIntosh Family of Camden and McIntosh Counties, Georgia, and Alachua and Duval Counties, Florida: Four Generations of Plantations and Politics." Typescript, April 17, 1998. Department of History, University of North Florida.

Williamson, Joel. *New People: Miscegenation and Mulattoes in the United States.* New York: Free Press, 1980.

Wood, Wayne W. *Jacksonville's Architectural Heritage: Landmarks for the Future.* Jacksonville: University of North Florida Press, 1989.

Woodson, Carter G., ed. "Free Negro Owners of Slaves in the United States in 1830." *Journal of Negro History* 9 (January 1924): 41–85.

———. *The Mind of the Negro as Reflected in Letters Written During the Crisis, 1800–1860.* New York: Russell and Russell, 1969 (reprint of the 1926 ed.).

Wooster, Ralph A. "The Florida Secession Convention." *Florida Historical Quarterly* 36 (April 1958): 373–85.

Index

After forty-seven years as a teacher and college professor, Daniel L. Schafer retired from the University of North Florida in December 2007 as Distinguished Professor of History, emeritus.

His publications include two film series and many articles and books. His recent books include *William Bartram and the Ghost Plantations of British East Florida* (forthcoming 2010), *Thunder on the River: The Civil War in Northeast Florida* (2010), *St. Augustine's British Years: 1763–1764* (2001), and *Governor James Grant's Villa: A British East Florida Indigo Plantation* (2000).

With the help of students at UNF, he also created "Florida History Online," a digital history archive posted at the University of North Florida (www.unf.edu/floridahistoryonline/).

Books of Related Interest

Also from University Press of Florida

Slavery in Florida: Territorial Days to Emancipation,
by Larry E. Rivers

Colonial Plantations and Economy in Florida,
edited by Jane L. Landers

Black Voices from Reconstruction, 1865–1877,
by John David Smith

Fort Mose: Colonial America's Black Fortress of Freedom,
by Kathleen A. Deagan and Darcie MacMahon

The African American Heritage of Florida,
edited by David R. Colburn and Jane L. Landers

An American Beach for African Americans,
by Marsha Dean Phelts